Community Music:
A Handbook

Edited by Pete Moser and George McKay

Russell House Publishing

First published in 2005 by
Russell House Publishing Ltd.
4 St Georges House
Uplyme Road
Lyme Regis
Dorset DT7 3LS
Tel: 01297 443948
Fax: 01297 442722
Email: help@russellhouse.co.uk
www.russellhouse.co.uk

British Library Cataloguing-in-publication Data:
A catalogue record for this book is available from the British Library.

ISBN: 1-903855-70-5

Design by Spacelounge
Layout by Four23
Printed by Alden, Oxford

About Russell House Publishing

RHP is a group of social work, probation, education and youth and
community work practitioners and academics working in
collaboration with a professional publishing team.
Our aim is to work closely with the field to produce innovative and valuable
materials to help managers, trainers, practitioners and students.
We are keen to receive feedback on publications and new ideas for future projects.
For details of our other publications please visit our website or ask us for a catalogue.
Contact details are on this page.

Contents

Acknowledgements

This book would not have been created and MMM would not be the company it is today without the dedicated work of Company Manager, Kathryn MacDonald. Administrators rarely get the pleasure and satisfaction of completing projects into performance or publication and also rarely receive their rightful praise. Thank you.

At MMM thanks are due to the fantastic core team of musicians— Geoff Dixon for all the technical support and drinks at the Tivoli after the derigs from the training weekends—Judi Wright for her clear thinking, and organisation—Ben McCabe for his rhythm, humour and sensitivity— Rick Middleton for the training weekend CDs, and Dave McGinn and Keri Brocklebank for admin support.

At Spacelounge, Annamarie Lightfoot has yet again created a visual feel in this book, built on years of creative graphic design work for MMM (www.spacelounge.co.uk). Thanks also to Warren and Darryl at Four23 who took on the creative layout for the book using Annamarie designs and delivered on time with good humour and patience.

Geoffrey Mann at Russell House has also been a great support in MMM's first publishing adventure.

Finally thanks to the MMM Board of Trustees who have given us such trust and support over the last four years—Fiona Gasper, Ingrid Kent, Gary MacClarnan, Oliver Plunkett, Diane Sammons and Katherine Zeserson.

The book project has been made possible through specific funding from Arts Council England and Youth Music. At ACE over the years, MMM has received great support from Debra King, Eddie Thomas, Andrew Korn and Michael Eakin. At Youth Music we have had inspiring support from David Sulkin, Sally Stote and the whole staff. Thank you. MMM also receives regular funding from Lancaster City Council and Lancashire County Council which has enabled the company to carry out the ongoing long term development work in Morecambe and across Lancashire.

The content of the book is the result of ten years work that has gathered ideas and practice from a huge number of musicians and trainers including Beth Allen, Saphena Aziz Manjeet Bakhar, Steve Berry, Jeff Borraidaile, Wendy Brown, Dave Camlin, Sean Canty, Francisco Carrrasco, Duncan Chapman, Richard Chew, Mat Clements, Sian Croose, Josefina Cupido, Sam Dale, Bosco D'Olivera, Tim Fleming, Inder Goldfinger, Deidre Gribbins, Paul Griffiths, Carol Grimes, Sylvia Hallet, Tony Haynes, Dave Hassell, Gary Jarman, Isabel Jones, Johnny Kalsi, Loz Kaye, Mary Keith, Mpho, Heidi Manning, Bex Mather, Avtar Singh Manku, Keith Morris, Mark Newport, Angie Palmer, Ken Patterson, Andrew Peggie, Jan Ponsford, Mick Routledge, Amanda Quigley, Simon Steptoe, Tyndale Thomas, Jane Wells, Andrew Williams, John Woodward, Robert Worby.

On a personal level I would like to thank John Fox, Boris Howarth and Adrian Mitchell for their extraordinary artistic, poetic and conceptual inspiration over the last 24 years.
P.M.

When the editing of this book was most in my mind, in the summer of 2004, I met up again with some of the 'old-timers' from Community Music East in Norwich, at the 'tramp camp' behind the sand dunes at Waxham. With our kids round the smoking camp fire I heard you play some beautiful music, and we swam with the seals in the sea. CME was so good for me in the mid-1980s - twenty years ago! - and I acknowledge that with gratitude and pleasure.
G.M.

Preface
Pete Moser and George McKay

Listen.

Just stop talking for a minute and listen.

What do you hear?

It could be a groove on a record, a guitar riff, the ambient sound of the room, a group learning a new song, or a violin melody, but it's music…. Today, music workshops are happening all around us, in schools, community centres, day centres—a whole variety of venues—with people of all ages and backgrounds.

In fact, community music is one of the striking success stories of the community arts movement in Britain. This means that it features different advocacies and practices—how could it be otherwise with the many vibrant and committed social and cultural personalities who have invented it and stuck with it through thick and thin? Part of community music's energy comes from its different voices, many of whom are heard through this book, directly, or in quotation, or in echo.

This book originates from one particular community music organisation, More Music in Morecambe, and then moves out to acknowledge, discuss, embrace other inspiring and dedicated projects around the country. Partly the book stands as a celebration of the success of community music. It has been written after ten years of running workshops in the community, and ten years of creating training weekends for people who make music within their communities.

It is very much a handbook—it includes practical exercises, advice and guidance. It is intended to be accessible to and usable by a wide variety of musicians and community artists, so as well as the written chapters themselves, the book includes graphics, photographs, history, poetry, pictures and references to other books. It tells how particular musicians found their ways in to working in community music, and what actually goes in music workshops whether for singers, DJs, rock bands, percussionists, special needs groups.

All the writers have taken their own stories as a starting point for discussing workshop practice, with the idea that by reading and using the book other people can transform their history and enthusiasms into their own individual practice. It is a 'how-to' book.

We hope you enjoy it, use it in teaching, argue with it, add your own ideas to it, use the resources at the end to explore further. We hope it has a place on both your book case and your music stand.

POTENTIAL

Each cloud wants to be a storm
My tap water wants to be a river
The match wants to be an explosive
Each reflection wants to be real
Each joker wants to be a comedian
Each breeze wants to be a hurricane
Each passing thought wants to be essential
It's not just what I feel - it's the potential,

Each laugh from the throat wants to burst from the belly
Each yawn wants to hug the sky
Each kiss wants to penetrate
Each handshake wants to be a warm embrace
Each melting icecube wants to be a glacier
Each wave wants to be the smooth stroke of a forehead
Each cry wants to be a scream
Its not just what I see - it's the possibility,

Each carefully pressed suit wants to be creased
Each midnight frost wants to be a snow drift
Each mother wants to be a friend
Each night time wants to strangle the day
Each wave wants to be tidal
Each subtext wants to be a title
Each winter wants to be the big freeze
Each summer wants to be a drought
Each polite disagreement wants to be a vicious denial
Each diplomatic smile wants to be a one-fingered tribute to tact
Don't you see how close we are to crashes and confusion
Each drizzled rain wants to be torrential
It's not just what I see - it's the potential.

chapter 1
ways into workshops
by Pete Moser

OK, where do I start?

am I Pete, Peter, the one man band, Mr Moser?

where do I stand in the room?

how have I arranged it, what's at the centre of focus?

myself, the instruments, the chairs?

and am I in the right gear, was the T-shirt the right one?

how do I want the people to react when they come in?

do I want to be one of them, an outsider, perceived as strange, odd, hip?

can I change the lighting, is the sun shining behind me so it's a strain to look in my direction?

how many people are going to come in, are there enough chairs and are they in the right places so that the arrangement helps the session?

is it too warm or cold, how do I change the temperature?

will I need the extension, is all the equipment tested?

what will I start with?

are the instruments out or hidden in a bag in the corner?

It was worth getting here an hour early to sort all this out and talk with the staff here...now I have a much better feel of the session.

That's just a bit of it—the questions and thoughts before even one person has come into the room, and all of those and many more change for every session, group and project. The logistics, the practicalities start before that moment, with the pre-planning that defines the physical needs of a session. And that pre-planning defines the aims and objectives of the session and the context in which it is being placed. And once you are there and doing it, the decisions have to be fast, flexible and enable the group to fulfil its purpose. And most of the decisions are similar to the ones you make in real life—it's really quite like what you do anyway.

The following pages aim to start you thinking, to open a dialogue, to inspire you to create your own method of practice. They deal with six areas of workshop techniques that I have learned to be really important:

- Building relationships
- Warm-ups
- Logistics
- Positive learning
- How groups work
- Planning

All of the photographs were taken on More Music Morecambe projects and training workshops.

The chapter concludes with a series of top tips about running workshops, gathered from experienced workshop leaders and other sources.

Building relationships

Circles

In a circle everyone is equal, people can't disappear, and they have to engage with the activity

But people don't make perfect circles so, as a leader, don't position yourself on a flat side but at the point of the oval where it is easy to see everyone

A circle can be used as a starting point for a great number of games

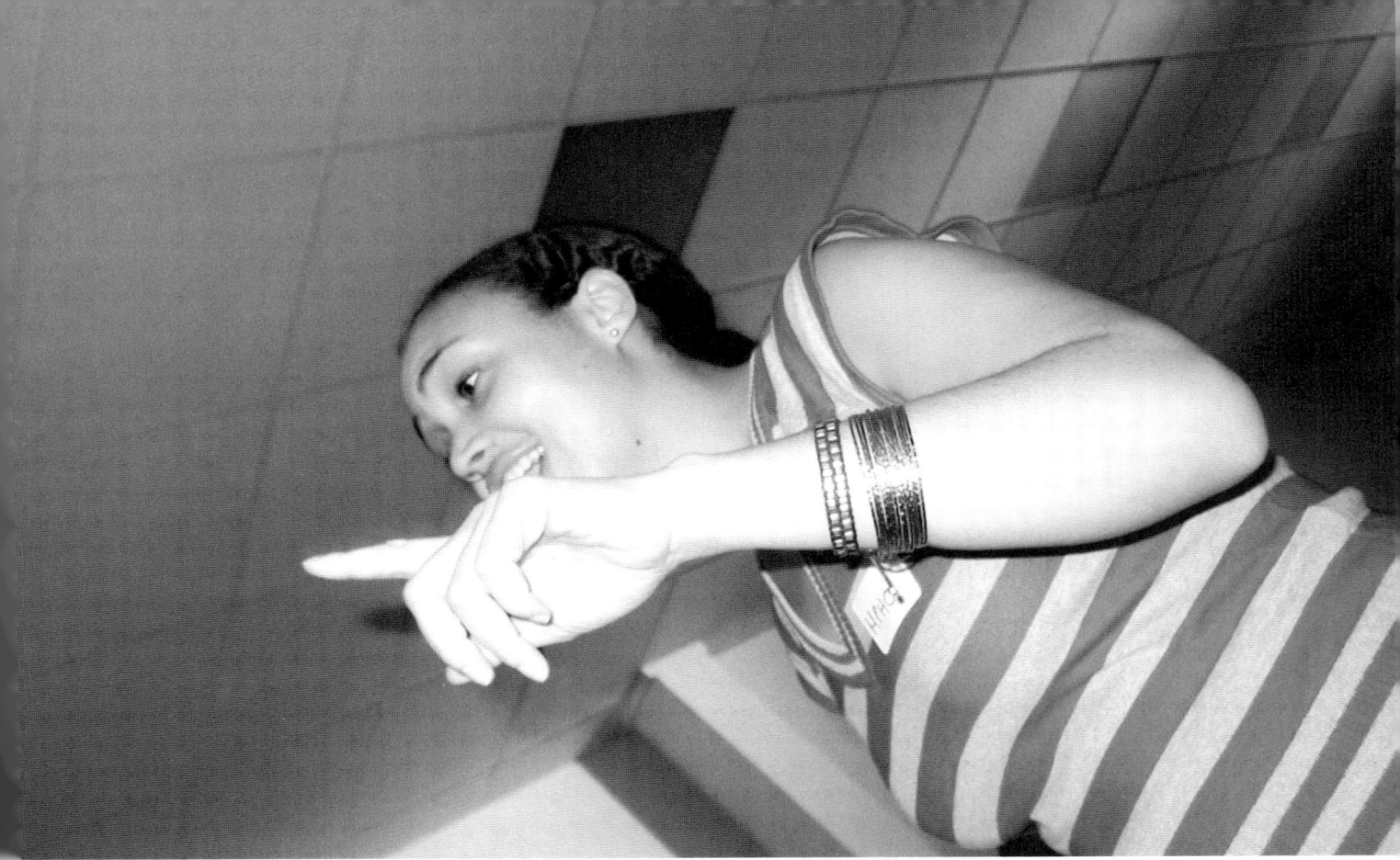

Trust

Gaining the trust of group is vital and helps everything move forward more quickly

People need to know that you understand and care for them, that you have experience and that if they trust you they are safe

The building of trust happens from the moment they walk into the room

Finding the right way to first engage with people is crucial

Clarity

Obvious but vital

Practice counting in and giving pitch
Try out a variety of hand signals and
decide which ones you like best

Be consistent, use the same gestures
so that your players gain confidence

Then you can play and change
volume, structure, orchestration and feel

Letting go

When a group starts to gel and
the content is right people will let
go and open in a very visual way

Music that involves obvious
physical movement often helps
to get things going

People can be so tense and
inside themselves that you
need any number of triggers

Laughter is always good for
loosening up but to get a group
going in the first place there
is a whole range of easy intro
warm-ups

Warm-ups

Body

Appropriate warm-ups relax the body,
move people away from habit patterns,
let go of some inhibitions and open the
flow of energy

Some groups will not want to warm up
but if you find the right warm-up it
transforms the session

Warm up the body and the brain

Warm up the group and the individual

Build up a repertoire

Drumming on chairs

Find warm-ups that give everyone an equal
place, that don't isolate or show up anyone
Warm-ups create focus and help to establish
a role for yourself as a leader

North East Warm-Up

This is a call and answer song written with
primary school children in Blaydon

Treat it freely, with fun

Add your own words to make it relevant to your group

Gett - ing rea - dy to dance, Getting rea - dy to cook. Gett - ing

rea - dy to kick. Gett - ing rea - dy to run. Gett - ing rea - dy to sing. Gett - ing

rea - dy to play. To day to day to day to day to day

Stretch our mus cles   Run a round the pitch   Jump an oc tave

Ba lance the scales   Bend our bo dies   Play a game do it

all a gain   Play a game do it all a gain

Logistics

The room

It is easy to take a space as it is given and
not consider what you can do to make it
better for you and your session

Many hosts don't encourage change
But Choose the right room
Work out the best focal point for you to set
up and lead from
Shift the furniture

Find appropriate chairs or cushions
Get the heating right, know how to control it
Maximise natural light to enhance the
atmosphere (strip lights are not conducive
to relaxed creative play)

Find where the lights switch on and off,
open the blinds

Clothing

Always think about what you are
going to wear and how you look

People do care and you can make things
a lot easier by thinking about it first

No need to go to extremes but consider
how you present yourself

Decide what you want to be called,
how formal do you want to be

Preparation

Being ready for a session can mean a great many things

This can range from lesson-planning to making sure your equipment is all working and in tune

It isn't good when you spend the first ten minutes of a session searching for a plug socket or looking for an extension or tuning your guitar

Arrive early to get ready

Positive learning

What creates a positive learning environment?
(this list was made on a weekend workshop. Add your own)

Simplicity

Variety

Feel good factor

A group that is open and receptive

A sense of achievement and ownership

Attractive equipment

Enthusiastic, non-judgmental leadership

A flexible plan with sensible activities

Musical progression and layering

Laughter to free the spirit and loosen inhibitions

Safety

Risk

Challenge

Individual space

Light

Patience

Teamwork

Clear communication

Well-explained boundaries

Listening

Smiles

It's a fact that the voice
opens when you laugh
The sound of laughter
relaxes the body, breaks
the ice, makes friends

Attention

It is usually easy to tell whether people are listening, engaged and have your full attention

Watch out for eye contact, body language and the amount of fidgeting

If you are talking for a long time and want people to listen well make sure that they are sitting down and comfortable

If the group is getting restless change the activity, use a number of different textures in your delivery to make sure that people stay engaged

Closed eyes wide open

As a leader you should try to use your eyes
to gather and reflect attention

With closed eyes we can listen more acutely
to music, less distracted by what we see.
Within a group some people feel uncomfortable
and vulnerable but it is worth trying. It opens a
new hearing world

You can use your whole body to teach

It's not just your hands but the whole shape of
your face and body that communicates what you
want people to do

Let your body respond to the music that you are
making and open those feelings and emotions to
other people in the group

How groups work

Groups are complex animals

Each has a character that is more than the sum of the individuals in it

Over time they develop and change; expressing anxiety, curiosity, establishing norms, engaging with the task, completing it and ending the group

Take a moment to step back and see your group as one single organism

What colour or shape would it be?

Or what sort of animal?

It's more obvious to notice how individuals are being—quiet, mischievous, and so on

Then there are the interpersonal dynamics too: 'those two seem to set each other off, these two seem to be getting on very well'

Remember all the time you are working things are going simultaneously at three different levels: individual, interpersonal and group

Engagement

There are so many different ways in which
people engage with a session

So many are just lost in the moment, experiencing
the music and atmosphere

Others stay a little outside the situation and
evaluate what is happening to themselves, worry
about their relationship to the group, question the
methods and process and judge the leader and
other participants

How do you make sure that
everyone is there in the room in body and mind?

The ones on the outside
Do you allow people to watch you run a workshop?
Do you eject those who aren't taking part, or who
are actually obstructive?

Celebration

Most people like to be noticed

For participants it is good for confidence and credibility
For a leader it is a useful way to celebrate an achievement
and enhance a group

A group photo focuses a particular level of energy
Recordings, certificates, press articles, speeches at the
end of gig—these can all work, too
There are many other ways

Going with the flow?

When do you push a group and challenge their expectations?

How do you ask them and talk with them about what they want to do?

Consultation is one thing but participation in decision-making creates a new ownership
Do you control everything from the start to the end?

Can you allow a few people in the group to take over the energy and flow of a session?
When is it right to let that happen and when should you keep tight control?

If you let it go can you get it back?

Planning

Defining aims

Who is the workshop or project for?

What is the activity?

What is the purpose?

What are the needs of the participants?

What is the time scale?

Who are the hosts, what do they want?

Thinking ahead

How much information do you need in advance?

Number/age range/gender/ethnic
background/special needs—are these important?

Their levels of experience

Their background as a group

The shape and the pace

Get the shape right—
Start easy

Draw people in

Attempt some tricky music

End with success

Sometimes sit back and let the group find its own way through a process but at times lead with an energy

What kind of atmosphere do you want? Chatty and informal, serious and didactic, physically energetic, full of humour and jokes, or a mixture of all of these?

Drums or decks

Some sessions will allow 20 people to take part -
working with drums or voices, for instance

Other sessions work best on a one-to-one basis -
like with decks or soundtech

Knowing this is important or you set yourself up with problems

A bag of tricks

Sometimes a session
is a single focus but it's always
useful to have another ten ideas
up your sleeve

A list of songs, games
and exercises

A set of different instruments

Talking of which, here are some top tips

They are taken from a variety of sources, the idea originating in some Ways Into Workshops weekend courses we have run at MMM over the years. We also had the Spitpot (Top Tips backwards) for bad ideas, but we're not going there. I then asked around for a few extras. Again, you can add your own.

Beautiful instruments
Beautiful instruments inspire. Collect a few special looking instruments that people really want to play but if something is really precious and personal be aware of who you give it to in a session. PM

Building strength
Sometimes you can only go so far in a session because people are physically tired. They have lost strength in their lips or forearm. Watch out for this and take a rest. PM

Chat up the caretakers!
Get to know them over a cup of tea or two. Leave them chocolate at Christmas. Seriously, with them on your side, life can be so much easier (getting in to the venue, arranging the room, trouble-shooting technical equipment). However, rub them up the wrong way and they can be just another headache. DC

Comfortable drums
Instruments shouldn't hurt. Get the straps right, or the right type of stick. Just as when you sing you need to sort your posture and body awareness so when drumming make sure the instrument is the right size for the body. PM

First session or sixth?
Most aspects of workshop leading change according to whether it is a first session or a point further along the way. Keep on your toes. WIW

Fact sheets
Have some fact sheets and technical language and know when to use them. MK

Fun fun fun
If it's something you enjoy doing, others will too. HN

Full body movement
It's fun when a drum rhythm involves a physical movement, if people are able. It looks good in performance and focuses a little group. But big movements sometime put people out of time with the groove so watch out. Balance the gesture with rhythmic accuracy and feel. BTB

Keep at it
Writing (composing) is like jogging. Many people will decide to start jogging and then after a week, they give up. It was hard, they're busy, there is so much to do. The fact is this: writing (composing) is like jogging—one hour a day can make the greatest difference and each time you will run further and further, not in time, in speed. It doesn't have to be an hour it can be ten minutes. LS

Knowing who to give instruments to
Create warm-up games and exercises that allow you to get an idea of people's skill levels. It can be demoralising having a group piece dominated by someone with an insecure sense of rhythm or pitch. Find easy ways of taking instruments away from people- suggestions that don't make people feel as if they have failed. PM

Listen broadly
Even if you have no intention of working in a particular genre, it's always worth keeping abreast of current musical tastes / fads (esp. when working with young people), as there may be ways of incorporating different musical styles / instrumentation into your practice (e.g. fusing rock instruments / decks with a drumming group). Tastes change: knowing your New Monkey from your Spanish Hardcore might be useful in 2004, but the landscape of youth culture is constantly shifting… DC

Reading (listening)
Feeds the subconscious writer and will enormously benefit your writing (composition), beyond your own predictions. LS

Making a set
When working with less confident performers it is important to give people confidence before they are out on their own. A mass piece to start followed by smaller groups can help to settle people in front of an audience. WIW

Mistakes
Making mistakes and looking at what happened are one of the chief ways we learn. Yet many people's fear of them can be almost disabling. Encourage people to welcome their mistakes. Be comfortable with your own. To quote that well-known chronicler of human frailty, Leonard Cohen, 'There's a crack in everything. That's where the light gets in'. SL

One-to-one
It is a great thing to allocate time for one-to-one work with people. The depth of personal exploration can be great but create the right setting or people will freeze up. LS

Outside
Sometimes it is right to move outside, to move to another room. It is great for the ears because they have to fit the sounds together in a different way with another kind of acoustic bouncing and mixing. PM

Ownership
Find ways of transforming other people's exercises and ideas to make them your own. MK

Partners
Engage the interest of others in the community (parents, teachers, youth workers, council Arts development officers, volunteers) to support the work. They can help to shape / steer the project, as well as help out with booking venues / coaches, driving, making the tea, sourcing funding… DC

Party piece
Have a party piece ready to inspire, to fill in when things fall apart. HN

Perform

Wherever possible, have some opportunity within a series of workshops to perform (either to each other, an invited or a public audience.) The 'buzz' (sense of achievement) participants get from performing will often be the impetus for continuing the activity. DC

Pitch

Always carry a means of pitching a note (pitch pipes, guitar, keyboard etc.) for vocal work. DC

Repetition

Know when to repeat things (repetition is how new learners learn best—essential for building confidence and learning technique) and when not to repeat things ('I'm sick of that song, that game'). DC

Struggle

If you are struggling with this then that is a good thing, the struggle is part of it, it's the pain barrier. LS

Struggle 2

Who told you that you couldn't do this. Was it an English teacher? Was it a parent? Was it a cleverer brother or sister? Finally I can guarantee that the doubts are yours—sometimes when you try and be creative you find yourself struggling with all these voices. Welcome to a newer you! Welcome to inspiration! LS

Tuning drums

A set of matched percussion instruments is like a small orchestra. They sound good in ensemble when they are tuned together and have a good range of sounds from low to high in pitch. BTB

Warm-downs

Consider the right way of ending a session. On occasions this might mean a physical warm-down, like a soft song. At other times a high energy finish, at others a silent meditation. WIW

Credits for top tips

BTB: Beat the Bay (percussion weekend)
DC: Dave Camlin
MK: Mary Keith
SL: Steve Lewis
PM: Pete Moser
HN: Hugh Nankivell
LS: Lemn Sissay
WIW: Ways into Workshops (from MMM weekend courses)

FLOCK OF SOUND

There is a rhythm, a soul's rhythm
A come in from the cold rhythm
A no need to go rhythm
A take off your bruise shoes
And shake off tomorrow rhythm
There is a rhythm, a wild rhythm
An adult's just a child rhythm
A blissed out whispering
Smile while listening rhythm.

There is a rhythm, a higher than sky rhythm
The rhythm of spaces, a sweet tasting
Liquor laced rhythm. An eyelid flicking
Slick thigh licking rhythm
A come home from the comfort zone rhythm
A relax in your black and take nothing back rhythm.

There is a rhythm. A rhythm.
A sweet sounded grounded rhythm
A spaced out sense of place rhythm
A give in to your within rhythm
A rainy season body teasing
Dripping sugar caned cocooned
Landing on the moon rhythm
A making room rhythm.

A lake and mist lip kissing dew glistening
Earthed and wired surround sound future bound
Magic carpeted and homeward bound rhythm
A pain soothing hip moving pressure releasing
Depression decreasing graffiti wriggling baby
Giggling zebra crossing—walk don't walk—button pressing
Up town down town dressing spirit shaking earth quaking
Ripples in a lake of a rhythm
Ripples in a lake of a rhythm
Ripples in a lake
A flock of sound.

chapter 2

Drumming, silence and making it up

by Steve Lewis

Also BoomDang: a case study by Dan Fox

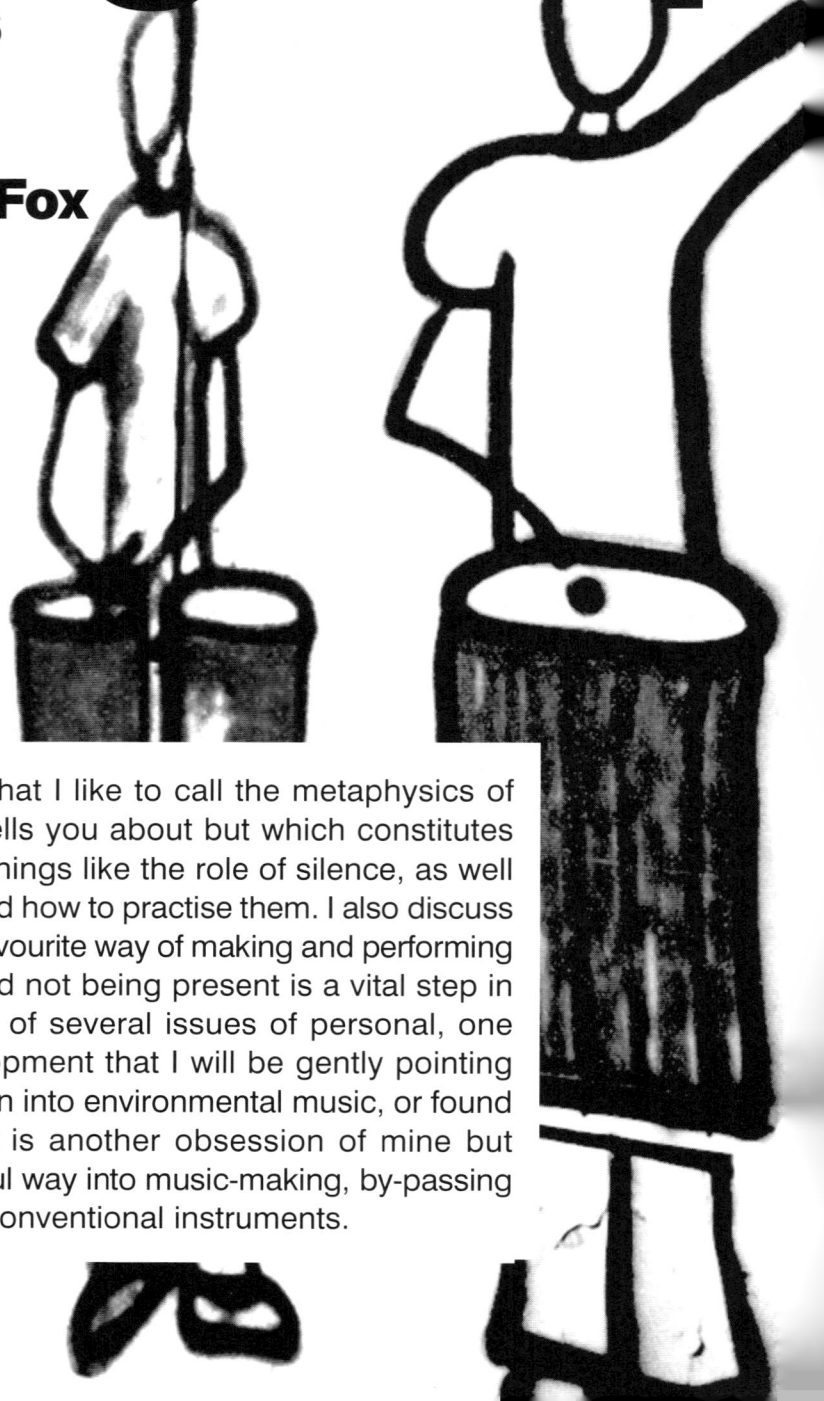

This chapter is a story about what I like to call the metaphysics of rhythm—the stuff that no-one tells you about but which constitutes the DNA of music. This means things like the role of silence, as well as listening and concentration and how to practise them. I also discuss improvising because that is my favourite way of making and performing music. Learning about being and not being present is a vital step in the art of improvising. It is one of several issues of personal, one might even say spiritual, development that I will be gently pointing up. Also, there is a short diversion into environmental music, or found sounds, not only because that is another obsession of mine but because it can also act as a useful way into music-making, by-passing people's anxieties about using conventional instruments.

2

The ideas I am presenting are intended to be both practical and thought-provoking. My interest is in stimulating you to think about how you can help people make up their own music. I am also interested in helping you think more about what you bring as a musician and a teacher. This involves encouraging you to wonder about the self that does this teaching and playing, to bring mindfulness and reflexivity as well as a willingness to 'play' to all you do. While much of what follows is my own work I have been influenced by the work of others, especially the English drummer and teacher John Stevens, as collected together in *Search and Reflect*. I will also draw on things I have learned while teaching alongside other percussionists. The chapter closes (or opens up at the end) with some material by Dan Fox, in which he explains his particular route through percussion and community music.

The life-changing workshop (they do happen)

I once had a life-changing experience in the middle of a five-day residential intensive on conga drumming led by Dudu Tucci. We had spent two hours learning and practising a couple of complementary Brazilian grooves for three congas. Suddenly I realised I had had enough. And this had nothing to do with Tucci, who is a fine and inspiring teacher with lots of interesting things to impart, especially about performance and presence. What I realised was that I was not interested in being taught any more patterns. I was not even sure I ever had been. This provoked an existential crisis! If I did not want to play this stuff, still less teach it, maybe I was not a 'proper' drummer at all. And what did I want to do?

It also raised for me questions about technique, which I have s i n c e learned were being approached by other community musicians and percussionists in different ways. Technique per se has become less and less important to me, in both my playing and my teaching. But I do think it is a valid way of approaching rhythmic education, and I have the greatest of respect for different approaches. For instance, Bosco d'Olivera was brought up in Brazil learning the songs and rhythms of samba, bossa and candomble. That music flows through and out of his body like a first language. He learnt to play by watching and copying the people around him, professionals and just people playing on the street. Later on he listened to records and people like Airto and Nana Vasconcelos influenced his approach. He helped to found the London School of Samba in 1984 and presently works extensively with the percussion project Drumtech. D'Oliveira insists that you cannot play samba with a good feel unless you know the songs these grooves were made to accompany. This is his explanation too for the woodenness of so much of the music played by the plethora of samba bands in the UK. So he teaches the songs and even some of the movements that go with them in his workshops. You may be singing, dancing and clapping before he lets you near a drum.

I always try to give people something to think about. With Drumtech students I get them to think about how to adapt percussion parts onto kit. I try to get people to think about the overall thing. Not just patterns. Certain styles need certain patterns sure but it doesn't stop there. The patterns relate to songs where the melody is the most important thing. You have to know the tune and see how the percussion fits in around it.

Interestingly the most frequent criticism Bosco hears is that he is going too fast for people, assuming they know things that they do not. He has had to work hard to monitor this in himself and slow down. And in this he touches on what can be the one disadvantage of 'first-hand' teaching—the difficulty of teaching what you imbibed as much as learnt.

For myself out of that workshop experience with Dudu Tucci I came to see first and foremost I was and am an improviser. I like making it up as I go along. I am also drawn to the sounds of found objects. I hear as much potential for music-making in a radiator as a conga. I am fascinated by the physical, psychological, and spiritual power that rhythm exerts. I began to appreciate that for me learning and teaching patterns was only a means to an end. It is an excellent way of learning technique, and acquiring technique is an excellent way of developing confidence. And people, especially adults, need confidence before they will let themselves play in the fullest sense of the word. Playing, in the fullest sense, is what I believe people need to do to if they want to express and communicate something of themselves through music.

This has to do with understanding what interests you and what you are good at doing, knowing what you do and what you do not do. I am convinced that the deeper your work comes from inside you the more likely it is to impact on others. So find out who you are. Do not just pass on some samba groove that someone else has passed on to you because it seems easy or fills a gap. When you have enjoyed a workshop consider how that happened. Notice what moves you, what you derive joy from. Pursue that, refine it, pass that on.

Having said all that here is a taste of what I am about. It is an exercise to try that will take you and whoever you do it with straight through to the bricks and mortar of rhythm.

Sound Silence Sound

Clap your hands once.
What's that?
You can't tell. The question is meaningless. So is the sound.
You feel, perhaps, a little uncomfortable.

Clap again, this time twice.
What's that?
Maybe something. Still too soon to tell.
You feel, perhaps, a little curious.

Clap again—three times, leaving the same space between each clap.
Aha!
Now we're getting somewhere.
Repetition allows you to anticipate order and surmise certainty.
The beginning of a pulse.
You feel, perhaps, a little relaxed.

Clap again five or six times and make the spaces irregular.
Different experience?
Perhaps irritating, even unsettling?

Notice the claps are the same every time. They contain the same information, if you like. They tell you nothing about the rhythm. What makes it a pulse or beat or rhythm or groove are the silences, the spaces. It's what you don't play that creates the comforting, exciting pattern of rhythm. Actually it's both of course. I am exaggerating a little to make my point. I'm making a distinction between what you notice and what's in the background. I'm asking you to give some attention to what's usually left in the background and make that figural for a while. It's like that drawing where two faces frame a candlestick but you can't see both at once.

Focus on the faces and you lose the stick and vice-versa. According to John Collins, in *African Pop Roots:*

The space and silences between the sounds are as important as the sounds themselves—whether they are the void between the threads of cross rhythms, the gaps that pairs of rhythms leave for one another in their dialogue, or even the awareness of the binary impulses of each individual rhythm—the silent upstroke and played downstroke... The trick is to be able to flip at will from focusing on sound to focusing on silence, from figure to background.

In *Search and Reflect*, John Stevens has a piece which lets you play with spaces by jumping over them. A group of people set up the simplest pulse possible, each person saying either 'one' or 'two' as appropriate. Once the pulse is there, people are free to 'jump' to the other number. Like many simple musical ideas it is quite complex to explain but very simple to do. When people do it in pairs there is always a wonderfully disconcerting moment when both are suddenly on the same number and a gaping big hole appears in the unoccupied space! Stevens has given us a deceptively simple and mind-boggling experience direct from the quantum face of rhythm.

What is this thing called Rhythm?

Rhythm is corporeal. We use the word pulse which suggests the heartbeat. Musicians didn't invent rhythm. Rhythm is part of music because it is part of how we experience, organise and make sense of being alive. We actively look for patterns in the world. Patterns arise out of repeated experience to create cycles. 'Sound silence sound' is both the fundamental and the overarching structure of all cycles. It is all around us—not just the heartbeat but the very act of breathing, day and night, seasons. It is so deep within us we cannot exist without it—think of the rhythms of sleep, hunger, solitude. The beat in its predictability makes a comforting salve against the uncertain and the unknown: 'What next? Who knows! Ah good. This again.'

By the way watch out for all those words we use—pulse, beat, rhythm, groove. So often we use them interchangeably when they mean different things. I once worked in a trio with a pianist and soprano player. We had lots of disagreements about playing rhythmically. One day I noticed something. When the piano player talked about rhythm he meant playing music with a pulse. For him, rhythm = beat. I think beat and pulse can be used as synonyms. Both are like fence posts in making sense of sound. Perhaps the pulse is evident when a beat is not tangibly marked. Likewise the beat is the pulse made manifest. But for me, rhythm = groove—a particular arrangement of sounds and spaces within a beat. This is often, but not necessarily, about repetition, and usually something that influences me to move my body.

The soprano player was talking about the rhythmic structure of melodic statements—about phrasing. This introduces another simple but much overlooked phenomenon. Rhythm is melody and vice versa. You can take them apart to try and analyse them but in action they are inseparable. By melody here I mean tune, pitch, timbre, dynamics: the component parts of phrasing. There is no melody that is not rhythmic and no rhythm that cannot be sung. (Many percussion instruments, like tabla drums, are taught by singing the rhythms). Think of a riff—a cyclical rhythmelodic phrase. Or listen to the rhythmelodic envelope of your own speech patterns. And of course rhythm has to be phrased. So, no wonder the three of us could not agree. We were discussing three intimately connected but quite different concepts. Be sure you know what you mean when you use these words and what the people you are working with mean, too.

Five ways to concentrate on listening

The first word of the endlessly reinventing jazz trumpeter Miles Davis's autobiography is: 'Listen'. It is an imperative. I am not a virtuoso musician and never have been, but I am good at listening. (The same basic ability took me into the world of psychotherapy, but that is another story.) There is a skill that is even more basic which is fundamental to good listening—concentration. I often feel when I am running workshops, especially in schools, that I am not doing music at all. Or rather music is just a means to an end. And the end is concentration. I find I am running classes in how to concentrate. Here are five ideas as much about concentration as listening

1. Count to Ten

This is a good demonstration of why people need to concentrate and listen. Click a tempo (another word you must know what you mean by. I mean a pulse with one consistent speed) of about one beat per second. Get a group of people to count in that tempo to ten. They have to do it in their heads, silently and without moving their hands or feet. So you might click your fingers four times to mark the tempo then say 'One' and everyone has to count silently to ten. When they get there everyone shouts out 'Ten!' And that's it. Insist there is no right or wrong to this—it is simply an experiment or a demonstration. You will find everyone arrives at a different time. Sometimes there can be as much as four seconds difference between the first and last. Ask the group what they make of the experience, especially the differences. What I make of it is that it illustrates beautifully how each of us runs to a different rhythm (maybe connected to metabolism). If these are so different that within ten seconds we can be so far out of sync with each other, ask them to imagine if we had carried on f o r several minutes. In classical music, conductors solve this problem. In most of the music I have played the only way round it is for everyone to listen listen listen. When everyone is listening people will almost unconsciously adjust to create an unspoken consensus about the group tempo.

2. All Clap

Ask everyone to start clapping a beat at the same moment. No discussion, just start. Notice what happens. At the outset this should sound like random noise. Quite soon a clear beat will emerge and very soon after that everyone will be clapping the same beat. Now discuss!
If one or two people are still clapping their own beat at the end you'll probably find they've been determinedly not listening—which is a skill in itself. Eventually of course you need to hear the whole groove without being drawn into what others are playing. In West Africa the tendency to find yourself playing your neighbour's pattern instead of your own is called 'sweet ears'!

3. Phenomenological Focussing

Yes, I know, but I am afraid I just love the sound of these words! This term comes from Gestalt psychology where it simply means noticing what you notice. In music workshops I use it as a way of grounding people in basic listening (and concentration). It works best in pairs. Each pair takes themselves off somewhere slightly separate from the others. For a short time—five minutes, max.—one person listens and describes to their partner whatever they can hear as they hear it. For instance, 'I can hear the computer fan whirring, feint whoosh of traffic, something high-pitched in my ear....' No chat, just description of what is being heard. The partner's job is just to hear what is being described and keep them on task. After the five minutes they change round.

This usually gives people (of all ages and musical expertise) a deeper experience of their aural environment than they are used to. They will often report hearing things they had never heard before. If you're lucky it will give them a quite radically new experience of what can be got out of simply listening, which they will then be willing to feed into their playing. Do be careful with this if you try it in the 'graveyard slot' (immediately after lunch). People can fall asleep!

Try it for yourself right now (it doesn't matter if you haven't got a partner) and notice what you notice about what there is to be heard.

4. Hocket

Hocket is a term for an extraordinarily collective way of making music used in traditional cultures all around the world. I use it as a way of getting people to listen to spaces. It works by each person having just one sound to make. When everyone puts their sound in just the right place at just the right moment a tune/groove/phrase emerges. No one person plays it—the whole group has to work together to make it happen. Imagine 'Happy Birthday' sung in hocket by four people taking a syllable each:

A: Ha
B: Pee
C: Birth
D: Day
A: To
B: You

C: Ha
D: Pee, etc.

In small-ish groups to begin with (five or six participants), using any sort of percussion, get people to choose one sound each. One at a time they make their sound which also involves having to make a decision about how much space to leave between theirs and the preceding sound. Once everyone's made their sound the first person starts again and the group keep up a constant loop. They will hear a riff emerge but only if they pay close attention to the spaces between the sounds and keep them the same each time. Give them a few times round to adjust to the sounds and the spaces, then insist that they try and keep it regular. It can help if you give them a beat to relate to but discourage them from clinging to this.

Once they've got the hang of it and made a working hocket you can get them each to learn the group phrase, maybe add others to it, and then point out that they've made a group composition that does not belong to any single one of them. You could also use it as the starting pattern for 'Add-On' and 'Rhythmic Improvising' below.

5. Add-on

If hocket works horizontally, then this works vertically, stacking rhythms on top of each other. The opening rhythm can be produced in many different ways. It can just be made up there and then or a hocket used as above. I've seen people use student's names, addresses, random phrases from newspapers—anything. One person begins by playing a simple rhythm. The simpler the better—complexity can be built in later on. The next person adds something to the first rhythm that is not the same but helps the first one groove and so on till everyone's in. Once you're in you have to keep going. Making your own foot tap is the order of the day—if the group can get itself dancing so much the better.

If this works well you can move on to the second stage which follows the same structure but once everyone is in anyone can change what they're doing whenever they like. Copying or improvising from what others are doing is allowed too. Insist that to change they have to first stop, then listen to what's happening and only come in once they've found something to play.

Environmental music

When you were phenomenologically focussing what did you hear? People talking, wood creaking, traffic? Whatever it was, would you call it music? If not, why not? Next time you listen to a recording of some 'music' notice how you listen. What do you attend to? What makes it music to your ears? If this is difficult turn the music off but maintain the same mode of attention to what you hear in its place. You are now creating environmental music.

I believe, and I'm not on my own here, that everything in the aural field is musical if you listen to it as if it were music, with an aesthetic ear, let us say. This applies not only to what seems pleasing or beautiful—the melody of a bird, the rhythm of the sea—but also the vacuum cleaner or a low-flying plane. Next time you are cleaning the house configure the vacuum as drone and try singing over it.

This is not just about noticing sounds, of course. The world is one big sonic resource and anything in it is a potential musical instrument. I have a lot of fun going round knocking, plucking and blowing whatever looks promising. This attitude has had a seriously deep influence on my music-making and how I run workshops. Playing a table, a coat stand, or a tumble drier can be liberating for people who do not believe they can 'play' with 'real' instruments. One of the beauties of this is that you can do it anywhere even with no equipment. I once had a group of people playing a stream—it was quite wonderful and proved to me that, if you ask them nicely and with conviction, people will follow you just about anywhere.

Find a Sound

Wherever you are—classroom, living room, stream—ask people to explore the sound-making potential of that place and what is in it. You might want to preface this with a demonstration of what strikes you as sonically interesting. Then let them roam for five minutes or so.

Once they've located an object ask them to fix the sound they like. Notice what you hit something with is as important as what you're hitting. Encourage them to try different sorts of sticks, beaters, hands, fingers, cutlery, knitting needles, and so on. Get them to think about dynamics, duration, timbre.

Now you can start playing. I find Hocket a particularly good starting place and you can move onto any of the rhythm ideas from the previous section. Or any of the improvising ideas in the next section.

Improvising: starting and stopping it

People can be very anxious about beginning to improvise. The important thing to get over is that they cannot make a mistake. You can talk about how and why you liked or disliked what somebody played but you can not really say 'You got that wrong'. If they look at you doubtfully, suggest they think of their mistakes as opportunities. So encourage, persuade, or cajole people into just having a go. The more reluctant they are the more they are likely to find it personally liberating. Scribbling is a great way to begin. Another John Stevens idea, it is the aural equivalent of doodling. It works by getting people to make sounds without their paying any attention to what they are doing—by-passing their critical egos if you like.

Scribbling

There are three stages to scribbling. First ask people to make a fast continuous noise on their instrument as a way of giving the others in the group something to listen for. Each person pays no attention to what they are playing. Their attention is totally focussed on the sounds they can hear—everyone else scribbling. You can do this in pairs or in groups. You can suggest people use their breath as an initial focus ('Scribble on the exhale. Silent on the inhale'). The second stage is for each person to notice the sounds they are making as well as the 'whole' scribble without changing what they are doing. Finally players can begin to control what they are playing and respond to what is happening. By now of course they will be involved in a group improvisation.

Improvising means making it up as you go along. I am always amazed by people who say they cannot improvise. After all, aren't most of the conversations you ever had completely improvised? In music you can use a theme or structure of some sort, like a particular tune or a 'blues', or you can play completely free. I am a fan of the latter. Here's soprano sax jazz player Steve Lacy talking about the first time he tried it at the behest of the late great trumpeter Don Cherry:

He used to come over to my house…and tell me. ' Well let's play'. So I said 'OK. What shall we play?' And there it was. The dilemma. The problem. It was a terrible moment. I didn't know what to do.

Starting can indeed be a terrible dilemma when there's nothing specific to play. That's where 'scribbling' can be so helpful. The thing is to just start. Play something and then listen. Or wait and listen. And you will have to try this for yourself. It won't be enough to read this and then go out and lead a session. I would say the quality of any group improvisation is determined not so much by technical skill as by the quality of listening made manifest in sound. So listen to the sounds around you, to other musicians, to the environment. Notice what you respond to and where from in yourself. Take yourself and/or your workshopees through the process of considering the following sorts of questions:

Are feelings aroused in you? Are you irritated, excluded, enchanted? How will you express that in sound? Think of it as a conversation— have your say. Can you listen and play simultaneously? Does a call-and-response structure emerge? Keep listening. *If you realise you've stopped listening, stop playing.* I cannot emphasise this last point too much. I have been amazed about how liberating people find it to be given permission to stop during an improvisation.
Indeed finding a way to end can be the most challenging part of any improvisation so that musicians can seem almost afraid to stop. Maybe they feel a responsibility to the others: we all have to support each other by soldiering on. But if nine people stop and one continues the piece still goes on. Indeed no-one can be playing and the piece can still continue if the quality of listening is there.

Without wanting to turn all zen-ish on you it is about being here. Group improvisation works when all involved are fully present. Rehearsing can be thought of as an exercise in mindfulness. If you find yourself daydreaming, if you are bored, if you have got nothing to say, stop. Listen. Then come back in when something energises you again. If this does not happen—stay out. That way you will help the group find an ending. Listen too for space in the music. Think contrast as well as complementarity. If everyone is playing fast consider playing slowly. People often begin to improvise like kids playing football, everybody following the ball. Good improvisers, like footballers, learn to make and use space.

'Freespace' is a deceptively simple score by Stevens. It can be quite challenging to play and is a useful one to try if one or two people are dominating a group. Begin with everyone listening to the relative silence of the room (phenomenological focussing, in fact). The group then starts, using whatever environmental sound there is as part of the piece, and playing together at a volume that allows that sound to remain audible. I have a great memory of leading a version of this piece with Pete Moser, Simon Steptoe and 30 others on the Hallé Gamelan. After a tentative beginning everyone was well into it, playing with considerable concentration often on the brink of silence. As momentum built again, Moser turned to me and mouthed 'How shall we end this?' 'Just wait', I whispered sagely, though I had no idea of what might happen. We waited and after another three minutes 30 people came to a clear end. There was a second's silence and we all burst into a loud cheer. It remains one of my most satisfying musical experiences—sometimes you really can 'trust the process'.

Five Easy Paths: rhythmic improvising

This is a model for helping people work out how to begin inventing their own variations on a given rhythmic theme. The emphasis is on starting simply. Just one change to a given phrase can be enough. It works particularly well as a development of Hocket. If you get the group to learn how to play individually the whole hocket they've created together, then they have a phrase to play with. Or you can just teach them a phrase. In this example, the phrase they have is 'took de-de ken'. I have five different options I can explain and work with a group on.

omission—leave out one of the beats:
' - de-de ken - de-de ken'

addition—add just one beat to the phrase:
'took de-de-deh ken took de-de deh ken'

displacement—shift the place of one beat:
'took dede ken took dede ken':

dynamics—make some of it louder or softer:
'took de-de ken took de-de ken'

internal looping—loop a small part:
'took de-de de-de de-de de-de de-de de-de de-de...'

As you get better at improvising you might want to experiment with holding back on your impulses. Do not always say the first thing that comes to you. Wait until you have something you actually want to say. Then wait until you have to say it. Try making up something with these words. Say, sing, drum or play them paying close attention to their meaning as well as whatever rhythmic and melodic shapes you may find.

Wait...

Wait until you have no choice.
Wait...

Decide to let what has to happen
happen.

Wait until you have to.
Wait...
Decide to have no choice.

BoomDang: another approach to community percussion

Dan Fox grew up as part of the performance and ritual theatre company Welfare State International where music and creativity was part of the culture. At a very young age he was playing with the professional musicians who came to work with the company from Africa, Asia and Europe as well as Britain. He picked things up hands-on working out intuitively what the people around him were doing. He learnt about offbeats and clave from a Nigerian musician. From Dutch musicians he learnt about non-standard time signatures. Only later did he check out what he had learnt from books. At the age of 14 Fox ran his first workshop at a WSI summer school, passing on the street percussion styles he had by now become so familiar with. He has gone from strength to strength developing a very particular vision that works well in mixed ability settings. The material he teaches comes from many different sources. He is not what he calls an 'ethnoanorak' but he does have particular things he wants to pass on and he does insist on using a particular structure to do that even if that does regrettably limit the range of experiences people might be introduced to. In his view, 'It's important to learn one rhythm straightforwardly. Then another. You may limit the possibility of surprising outcomes but you end up with a memory bank to improvise from. Otherwise you get lowest common denominator rhythms'.

The particular vision Fox has developed in his work is heavily influenced by his interest in design and making instruments. From years of playing street music he had very clear ideas about what he wanted from percussion, and what was lacking in the sort of kit you could buy. He recognised the importance of comfort and versatility. Since 1998 he has been perfecting the design and manufacture of his own double-sided drums which he's road-tested in bands like Boneshaker and Salt.

I take ergonomic factors into account for the design of the drums and the harnesses. I use mounting surfaces to incorporate mini hi-hats or sets of bells, which can be integrally tuned with the drums. All the drums are double-headed because that playing technique interests me, especially now I've made a midi version! And interestingly 99% of people assume I bought it all somewhere. They're very surprised to learn I made them.

That's it from me, but there's more now about percussion, from Dan.

BoomDang
a case study by Dan Fox

BoomDang drums are lightweight two-sided drums. The shells are made of birch plywood which is stained and lacquered with 3 layers of polyurethane varnish. The skins are plastic, the rings are aluminium and they are tensioned using polyester rope. This combination means the drums are both resonant and very light. An average samba surdo or bass drum of 50 cm diameter weighs about 7kg, whereas a BoomDang bass weighs 4kg. The skins are plastic so they are unaffected by the unpredictability of European weather. One skin is thicker than the other so the tones they produce have two pitches. The thicker skin producing a lower Boom sound and the thinner sounding higher, called Dang. The drums are carried with a balanced two shoulder harness. They are worn sideways so they do not bang your shins when playing them on the move.

The design and playing style are hybrids from many styles of drum from around the world. The original design concept came from Jos Zandvliet who is a Dutch musician, inventor and artist who created three drums of a similar design for a Dogtroep, a theatre company based in Amsterdam who specialise in site-specific outdoor shows. Many of their shows were performed to audiences of thousands of people with music by a four man unamplified band. Using drums, brass, gongs, tuned cowbells and other invented instruments it was necessary to create as loud a sound as possible in all kinds of weather. I worked with Dogtroep for five years until 1996. After I left I decided to make myself a couple of these drums. Since then I have been commissioned to make numerous other sets, for bands, arts organisations and a management training company. I have designed four sizes: bass 50 cm, tenor 35 cm, soprano 30 cm, and a 30 cm snare, which is played conventionally, not turned on its side.

The material below is from various sources. In 1997 I formed a four-piece percussion band called Boneshaker. This is a street band that performs with BoomDang drums, sound-making stilts, darabuka helmets and turntables. We play original material inspired by percussion music from around the globe. These road-tested grooves have formed the foundation for the teaching material of Furness BoomDang, which is a project that started in 2001. With funding and support from Youth Music and managed by The Sage Gateshead, Thérèse Johnston and I as Hands On Rhythm made a kit of 48 drums with sticks, bags and straps. Following taster sessions in local schools, nightclubs and youth centres we established regular sessions in Dalton and Barrow-in-Furness. This led in turn to four bands meeting locally on a weekly basis. We have performed locally and nationally, with some notable events being the opening of the Millennium Footbridge in Gateshead on BBC Music Live Day 2002 and a Royal Gala performance for the Queen in Newcastle. I encourage the young people I work with to compose their own material and I have included one of these rhythms.

Warm-ups

It is always a good idea to warm up your muscles before playing percussion. Warm-ups help to avoid muscle strain. The adrenalin you get when playing live can cause you to strain your body without noticing until afterwards. Warm up gently and at your own pace.
A few simple exercises before playing are:

• swing the arms in a circular motion, forwards and backwards
• shake the hands
• clap hands together then pat the forearms and upper arms
• interlink the fingers of both hands. Stretch the arms forward with the palms facing away from the body, then move up above the head, release the fingers and lower the arms down to the sides of the body.
• hold a pair of sticks in one hand a twist them back and forth at a fast speed for at least 30 seconds. Repeat with the other hand.

The material is for anyone interested in playing percussion. The notation and rhythms are designed for two-sided drums, but they can be adapted for percussion bands with other instruments. To play these rhythms on a single-headed drum, use a thin and a thick stick such as a "whippy" or a timbale stick and a solid wood drumstick or bass drum beater. Play the Boom sounds with the thick stick and the Dang sounds with the thin stick. The hi-hat that I refer to below is a mini hi-hat which can be handheld or mounted on the top of a drum. If you do not have one of these you could use cabasa or afuche instead. Although as you will see I have not notated a shaker part on any of the rhythms, shakers add a great drive to a percussion band and I would recommend that you use one whenever possible.

Score

A word about the three types of notation I use

1. Scores (see above): using a stave for each instrument, with the hi-hat and bell sharing one stave. The soprano, tenor and bass drums have two notes on each stave. In each case the lower of the two notes is always the Boom sound and the higher is Dang.

2. Mnemonics: word phrases and rhymes help you to remember a rhythm but they do not tell you which specific sound should be made.

3. Charts: these are boxes divided into 16ths of a bar with words describing a sound written on the appropriate beat. This is an adaptation of dhol/tabla notation.

Other words I use in chart notation are:

Ta (for hi-hat), Ka (for snare drum), and Kon (for cowbell).

Chart

Boo			Da	Boo		Da		Boo	Da		Da	Boo		Da	
1	2	3	4	5	6	7	8	9	10	11	12	13	14	15	16

Charts are useful for counting, to: use the shading of the boxes to help with counting. Try using your thumb on beat 1, first finger on beat 2, third finger on beat 3 and fourth finger on beat 4. Repeat this for boxes 5-16. To learn a rhythm count through the boxes using your fingers and say the words at the appropriate point.

Sweet potato

This rhythm is based on an Arabic darabuka rhythm often associated with belly-dancing. It is called 'Sweet potato' because this is the mnemonic used to describe the rhythm. It is a good earthy groove that gets people dancing, probably because the bass drum is playing a four-to the-floor pattern which is easy for a dancer to follow. The syncopation is made with the right hand, or Dnga skin. When learning or teaching this rhythm, it can be useful to start with the first half of the bar: 'sweet potato.' Introduce the second half 'I like potato' when the first part is solid. The snare pattern should be played hand-to-hand. The word phrase 'red pepper, red pepper' can be used to remember the snare pattern. See what happens if you push it to the no-man's land between straight crochets and a triplet feel.

Boo			Da	Boo		Da		Boo	Da		Da	Boo		Da	
1	2	3	4	5	6	7	8	9	10	11	12	13	14	15	16

Boo			Da	Boo		Da		Boo	Da		Da	Boo		Da	Da
1	2	3	4	5	6	7	8	9	10	11	12	13	14	15	16

Red		pep	red	red		pep	per	red		pep	per	red		pep	per
1	2	3	4	5	6	7	8	9	10	11	12	13	14	15	16

If it is solid, try playing 'Sweet potato' without the left hand or Boom sounds. This can work well as an introduction; the listener gets a false sense of where the one is. When the bass beat then comes in it takes a few moments to adjust. This happens sometimes in dance music: a DJ starts a record with minimal percussion and bass which is accenting the off-beat. The crowd dances believing they are boogieing to the on-beat but when the bass drum drops they are caught on the hop—literally. The dancers either fall over or do a quick hop step to get back on the one.

red pepper.....

sweet po ta toe   I like po ta toe

The break, which was composed by Ted van Leeuwen, is called the 'Time-out' and the signal for it is two hands making a T-shape. Keep the tempo solid and make sure the last seven beats are really tight otherwise it sounds sloppy. This break is played in unison by the soprano, tenor and bass drum. The snare, bell and hi-hat play their groove patterns but join in on the accents/boom boom.

Funky drummer

Everyone knows a version of this rhythm. It is one of the most common drum kit grooves. If you give a European a drum kit and a pair of sticks, this is probably the first rhythm they will have a go at. If you want to get into the feel of it, listen to some James Brown.

Soprano and Tenor

Boo		Boo		Da			Da	Boo	Da	Boo		Da			
1	2	3	4	5	6	7	8	9	10	11	12	13	14	15	16

Boo		Boo		Da			Da	Boo	Da	Boo		Da	Boo		Da
1	2	3	4	5	6	7	8	9	10	11	12	13	14	15	16

Tenor

Boo		Boo		Da			Da		Da	Boo		Da			
1	2	3	4	5	6	7	8	9	10	11	12	13	14	15	16

Boo		Boo		Da			Da		Da	Boo		Da	Boo		Da
1	2	3	4	5	6	7	8	9	10	11	12	13	14	15	16

Bass

Boo		Boo		Da			Da		Da	Boo		Da			
1	2	3	4	5	6	7	8	9	10	11	12	13	14	15	16

Boo		Boo		Da			Da		Da	Boo		Da	Boo		
1	2	3	4	5	6	7	8	9	10	11	12	13	14	15	16

The build-up is a device used in a lot of dance music. The snare and hand percussion keep a solid but light foundation with a strong backbeat. This can go on for a variable amount of time, for example, four or eight bars. When the double-sided drums come in it is with a strong unison beat. The sound should be like one drum. It is crucial to listen and count. This beat occurs four times over eight bars, then four times over four bars, four times over two bars, four times over one bar and finally eight times in one bar. This creates a 16-bar break in which the accented beat doubles its tempo four times.

The build-up is played in unison by the soprano, tenor and bass drums. The hi-hat and bell continue with their patterns, as does the snare except for the last two bars

Pineapple pie

This rhythm is in 6/8 time. The basic feel is three beats over two. To practice this play the following exercise with your hands on your thighs: both, right, left, right. Keep repeating this phrase until it flows smoothly. You will notice that your right hand is playing three beats in the same amount of time as your left plays two beats.

Cowbell

Kon			Kon			Kon			Kon		
1	2	3	4	5	6	7	8	9	10	11	12

Hi-Hat

Ta	Ta	Ta	Ta	Ta	Ta	Ta	Ta	Ta	Ta	Ta	Ta
1	2	3	4	5	6	7	8	9	10	11	12

Snare

Ka		Ka		Ka	Ka		Ka		Ka		Ka
1	2	3	4	5	6	7	8	9	10	11	12

Soprano

Boo	Boo	Da	Boo	Boo	Da	Boo	Boo	Da	Boo	Boo	Da
1	2	3	4	5	6	7	8	9	10	11	12

Tenor

Boo		Da	Boo	Da		Boo		Da	Boo	Da	Da
1	2	3	4	5	6	7	8	9	10	11	12

Bass

Boo			Boo	Da		Boo			Boo	Da	
1	2	3	4	5	6	7	8	9	10	11	12

Try playing the snare pattern with your right hand and the cowbell part with your left. The left hand is playing the same as in the exercise above. The snare pattern is a West African feel known as Bembe, originating from the word Bembes, which are religious gatherings that include drumming, singing and dancing.

Africa

Pine apple pie

Rhu barb pie

Bass variation. For this, it can be effective if the bass section drops out for a while. On cue, start the variation. When the phrase is solid you can try anticipating the Da beats. This pattern creates a more open rhythm in which a longer phrase is created.

APPLECART ART

Upset the art. Smash the applecart
Sell it for firewood to warm hearts
Don't join the loop the loop troupe
Don't hump through their hoops
Get stuck on sticky peaks of double speak
I'm clocking the click of the clique
I swim with the shallow
If they demand I be deep
Though I can hold my breath
Deeper than sleep, deeper than death.

Upset the art. Crash the Snapple cart
Sell it for cash and a brand new start
Turn cart wheels on the art wheels
If that's how your heart feels
To those who demand you stand by their pandect
Call them all cheats on call and collect
They're gargoyles hunched on their haunches
Stalking the walk at lunches and launches
They back bite back slap salubriously clap
With cleaver hands to stick in the back.

Upset the art. Trash the cattlecart
Start the stampede in the heart of the art
Don't play poker with the mediocre
Token filled pack full of jokers
The class A offenders are pretenders
Protecting their pretence return them to sender.

Feel fierce flocks of fight and flowing
Know you're only as good as your last poem
Cut yourself, it should be ink you're bleeding
You're only as good as your last reading
Let wisdom be the weight of your wealth.
And let your greatest competitor be yourself.

chapter 3

Improvisation and the development of community music in Britain

followed by the case of More Music in Morecambe
George McKay

Community is not something to be magically recovered but a goal to be struggled for. It is not something to be manufactured by outside professionals but emerges out of collaboration and shared commitment and expression. Cultural work is an effective tool in the formation of community, it is a tool for activism.

Gay Hawkins, writing of community arts in Australia

What is it that makes a musician important?... Is it in using his or her gifts, skills and experience to awaken and guide the dormant musicality of those whose music has been taken from them?... Once people become aware that music is in themselves and not only in those who have been selected to become musicians, once they take back to themselves the musical act in a spirit of delight and self-affirmation, who knows what else they might insist on reclaiming, and enjoying, of what has been taken from them?

Christopher Small, in John Stevens et al, *Search and Reflect*

3

The aim of this chapter is twofold. First, it traces the historical development of the idea of community music. It does this with particular emphasis on community music's relation to aspects of the 1960s countercultural project and its legacy. This involves looking at the role of free jazz in music education, links with the burgeoning community arts movement, the radical politics and social ideas frequently claimed by those central to community music. Community music remains imbued with the spirit of improvisation, and I think it important to acknowledge the special role played by that particular music (as opposed to, say, classical music outreach teams, grassroots folk or more recent world music projects) in its development. Second it narrates the development of the More Music in Morecambe community music project through the 1990s, its successes and (mini-) crises, its beliefs and practices. It considers the origins of MMM in some of the earlier musical/theatrical performance practice of Welfare State International, and locates MMM in the context of the rise of community music as a social-cultural phenomenon in Britain. This involves discussion of ways in which the radicalism or idealism of some of early community music has been knocked and/or maintained.

Community music in Britain: from improv to institution

Of course, as Anthony Everitt's *Joining In* demonstrates, there are many historical examples of participatory music-making in Britain, from factory- or coal mine-centred brass bands to those of the Salvation Army, from folk clubs with an amateur even DIY ethos (floor singing, regional music tradition), to hand or church bell ringing, choirs, steel bands, festivals, and so on. Similarly there are many precedents for the ideas of community arts—which Baz Kershaw has explored in *The Politics of Performance*. But, as with other areas of experimentation in life and culture, the events of one recent decade in particular do have to be acknowledged. According to Vicky White, a researcher working on community music at King Alfred's College, Winchester:

The 1960s could be regarded as the true beginning of the community arts movement and it sought to challenge the prevalent standards and assumptions about the value of art but found itself judged against them anyway….These pioneers wanted participation and relevance for the people as a whole. But they found themselves having to be judged within the standards set by larger organisations and funders within the dominant. Community arts grew up and were born in this atmosphere of a new age of defiance. It has been described as the 'socialist critique of capitalism'. The participants and instigators saw it as giving people a voice as it was used not only for social means but also for political demonstrations. It saw itself as anti-institutional and it used arts to effect social change.

Also during this decade a significant number of developments came out of the burgeoning European improvised music scene of the time. Politically this drew on the rhetoric of 'freedom!' of the times, and musically its influences were as varied as Cagean aleatory and silence, the African-American innovations of Ornette Coleman and free jazz, Asian and African sounds from the Commonwealth diaspora. In his book *Improvisation*, free guitarist Derek Bailey has argued that,

In England the first musician to run an improvising class was John Stevens. Stevens has always been a teacher. From the time in the middle 1960s when he emerged as the leading organiser of free music in London, having an idea, for Stevens, has been only a prelude to persuading his friends and colleagues to adapt it.

More importantly, for drummer Stevens, who would be centrally involved in important projects from the Spontaneous Music Ensemble in the 1960s to the successful establishment of the organisation Community Music in London in the 1980s, music workshops were an essentially social tool or space. The approaches being developed by Stevens at workshops and at the Little Theatre Club would be articulated most clearly early on in the liner notes for the SME album *Karyobin*.

The thing that matters most in group music is the relationship between those taking part. The closer the relationship, the greater the s p i r i t u a l warmth it generates. And if the musicians manage to give wholly to each other and to the situation they're in, then the sound of the music takes care of itself. Good and bad become simply a question of how much the musicians are giving.

Experimentation and musical change was for Stevens 'the only constant', and the political motivation for this was relatively straightforward: 'if people become more familiar with change, then automatically they become more tolerant as people'. From 1968 on Stevens was running music workshops for non-professionals— marked by a 1972 Thames Television Fellowship (for him and saxophonist Trevor Watts) for music within the community, in particular working with schoolchildren in Stepney, in the East End of London. He also ran what he termed Spontaneous Music Workshops at Ealing College in West London. Within a few years one of the activities of the proposed National Jazz Centre in London was outreach work, jazz education in the community, and from this grew the organisation Community Music, with Stevens as its Musical Director, in 1983. Both Community Music, and its offshoot project Community Music East, are still going strong today, though both have moved a long way from Stevens' purist improvisation and social music-making approach—though in 1997 Everitt can still refer to Community Music staff as 'missionaries' preaching the cause. This is seen in the fact that the band Asian Dub Foundation's 1999 album was called *Community Music*, for reasons explained by John Hutnyk.

The band's musical style was formed in the milieu of the music workshop located in Farringdon, and, as is often emphasised, in the East End of London: ADF's involvement with Community Music is more than as a contribution to an 'outreach' programme, but is explicitly linked to education, consolidation and politicisation work among youth of the East End. This work began with a programme in music making and media, MIDI techniques in a live situation, performance skills and mixing.

It is interesting to note that, for ADF, developments in music technology have been identified and employed for their social use (a point explored in greater detail in Rachel Healey's chapter). The politically and culturally radical ethos of community music, its 'socio-political overtones', as Everitt expresses it, is also maintained today by one of Stevens's early collaborators, the stellar improvising vocalist Maggie Nicols. As she told me in 2002, about a longstanding non-commercial commitment.

Every Monday night for twelve years we've been running what's got called 'the Gathering', a kind of informal musical, social workshop drop-in, in a room above a London pub. There's no fee, and no-one gets paid. It's not a workshop and I never say it is but people always assume it is. Improvised music is at the heart of it. The Gathering isn't fixed, it's fluid depending on who shows up, and that changes over time. The fact that it has lasted so long shows its value, and that it's needed, and that it is a long-term process, commitment. I've missed maybe ten nights in twelve years, which amazes me. It originates in my experience at a very frustrating London Musicians' Collective meeting, where there was some tension, bit of bad feeling, people wanting to go in different directions. I just said 'Wouldn't it be good if we could meet in a different way, maybe a gathering'. Sinead Jones, violinist and vocalist, said what a lovely word, better than a meeting. Loz Speyer (trumpeter) said we could bring instruments and trumpeter Ian Smith went out and found a pub for us to play in. The first evening no one was quite sure if we were there to talk or play and it was that very uncertainty that I feel has made it such an unusual combination of social and musical interaction. From that very first session it was totally inspiring. It was LMC members to begin with but it gradually widened out, and it's still going. The Gathering has a political dimension, it's creative, it's community. This is something important, an achievement. It feels like home.

Another important facet of the early identity of what was becoming known as community music was its uncertain place within the education world, existing as it did in the interstitial space between peripatetic instrumental teaching in schools, orchestral outreach teams, private lessons, youth and community arts work, music colleges and higher education institutions. In music education circles there has long been ambivalence about the place and method of teaching improvisation. For example, in his collection of writings, *No Sound Is Innocent*, veteran improvising percussionist Eddie Prévost has provocatively described the teaching of jazz in music colleges and universities as 'the flattening fifth'—a newer, fifth aspect of the scene that accompanies the original four (musicians, promoters, audiences and critics). In Prévost's punning view, formal education in jazz is counter to the intuitive improvised nature of the music, and can only produce what he calls 'brainless clones', all technique and idiomatic mannerism.

Betraying a certain insecurity, community music as education seemed to fall back on the kind of marginal identity cultivated by jazz in Britain. Stevens, for instance, could speak of 'professional musicians. I mean that in the bad sense'. Partly this was also a symptom of the anti-establishment aura building up around it, and perhaps too a residue of what Andrew Blake has called 'the aestheticised poverty' attitude within improvisation cultures. On the plus side, from jazz, community music learned how to hustle (in the sense of raise funds and survive, rather than the dance). In recent years, community music's outsiderdom in terms of the education system has been challenged. This is seen in the drawn-out debates about the relevance of accreditation (that is, the recognition by education qualifications of work experience in the field), while a number of universities and conservatoires now actually offer postgraduate courses in Community Music itself (York University, Ulster University, Birmingham Conservatoire, all offer Masters programmes in the field, for instance).

Yet, for all their radical rhetoric from the 1970s on, community arts generally relied on local and national government or arts organisations and sympathetic charities for funding. In the 1980s, for example, a national scheme called the Community Programme was a government initiative aimed at reducing registered unemployment figures by establishing projects across the community. (This could include anything from teaching water safety in schools to improvised music in youth centres, to providing gardening and landscape services in neglected parks or for families on benefit.) It was through the Community Programme that I was employed by Community Music East in Norwich, first as a musician, from 1985-1988. As I remember, salaries were surprisingly reasonable, and for some years a number of music and community arts projects worked within this scheme—no small subversive irony for many of those involved, since the Community Programme was an initiative out of the right-wing Thatcher administration. More recently, other pop music projects have gained funding under the Labour government's New Deal programme. Dave Price too remembers those times:

In 1989, community music often defined itself in oppositional terms. We didn't quite know what we were, but we were sure that we were not formalized education, nor were we anything to do with the dominant ideology. Indeed some of us (somewhat grandiosely, it must be admitted) saw ourselves as acting in open defiance of the Thatcher administration.... How things have changed.... It is a remarkable transformation, which has come about for a number of reasons, but perhaps the most significant being the willingness of the 1997-elected Labour Government to establish a dialogue with artists, educators and social scientists in addressing ... 'social exclusion'.... The ideas which emerged from that dialogue, however, could never have been implemented without the impact of the [funding opportunities made available by the] National Lottery.

The centrality of arts within the community is then recognised by government today as part of the equation seeking to address issues of social exclusion and regeneration, as a report to the Social Exclusion Unit for the Department of Culture, Media and Sport articulated in 1999: 'Arts ... are not just an "add-on" to regeneration work. They are fundamental to community involvement and ownership of any regeneration initiative when they offer means of positive engagement in tune with local interests'. This new language of community arts has indeed translated into concrete action so that in the past few years the quantity of community music activity across the country has developed impressively, with significant investment and support, and the recognition of the need for a network and infrastructure. Everitt speaks of 'the subsidy revolution' in this context. The investment in and expansion of community music has raised questions and problems for many of its early exponents—the evaluation and maintenance of quality services, how to move beyond the 'box of tricks' approach of individual practitioners, theorising one's practice, adjusting to expectations about training and accreditation, about budgets and grant applications, and so on. But, at the same time, the principles of community music as identified in 1990 at a conference of the International Society of Music Education—principles largely born out of the earlier idealism—are still recognisable in today's praxis. They are: 1. decentralisation, 2. accessibility, 3. equal opportunity, 4. active participation. In his book *Living Music*, Rod Paton places this in the context of our passive relationship to music and culture more generally. 'One of the major themes ... is participation, to which we might add related themes of ownership, empowerment and identity. We have become so used to consuming music that we are in danger of losing the capacity to make it'.

More Music in Morecambe
community music from community performance

Almost all of the work I do has a dual purpose. Community music for me has always been a mixture of being a social worker and a composer and finding ways of bridging that.... I passionately believe that music has the ability to make communities pull together.
Pete Moser

The director and founder of MMM, Pete Moser, lives in Morecambe, in a Victorian house on the sea front, with wonderful views across the bay, to the mountains and the sunsets. It is important for him to feel part of the community, and more, as he told me, to provide continuity and accessibility: 'for the long-term development of music participation, I like having worked with kids in a local school, then, when they are grown up, I've seen mums bring their toddlers, and, yes, I realise that I did work with them when they were at school. It's to do with people being able to see that music-making is integrated into everyday life, is part of normal experience, and absolutely not something separate or exclusive'.

He has an extensive background in music. In terms of formal education, he graduated in 1979 from Southampton University with a fairly traditional BMus (Hons). A chance meeting a couple of years later led him up to Ulverston in the Lake District, in 1981, to work with WSI. He worked as a technician and later a musician, initially voluntary but then paid, and in fact his first proper Welfare State gig—a true and typical Welfare State baptism of fire—was the now legendary 1981 bonfire night Parliament in Flames event in Catford, London. This, the final time for this particular show, did indeed include the burning down of the Houses of Parliament. Over the next five years Moser became musical director of the company, learning by shadowing existing MDs like Luk Mishalle and Boris Howarth, and gradually taking on most of the musical direction. Moser remembers that there was some freelancing going on round this time too: 'One Man Band stuff, and I also toured a show of poems and songs with Adrian Mitchell—I had a great sense of the politics being really out front with his work'. Mitchell's poetry and performance, and frequent blues-inflected lyrics, is ideally suited to musical accompaniment, of course.

Moser finished with WSI by doing a three-year residence in Barrow with the company, one of twenty arts animateurs established by the Arts Council round that time. 'That consolidated all of my thoughts about community music, performance, politics. It was an amazing time to be working in Barrow—right at the end of the Cold War, when a town like Barrow, built on defence and military industry seemed effectively to be made redundant'. After a kind of sabbatical, exploring world music and politics by working with the likes of Victor Jara's widow Joan in Chile, he returned to the north-west of England, in Morecambe. Why there? 'It was just round the bay [from Barrow]! Also it was a bit like Barrow, working class, familiar, but at a point when it needed to change, to have some energy and love put back in to it, and I could see myself contributing to that. And there was a small group of people, arts people, who wanted to work in the area as well, and that attracted me too'.

So, in 1993 Pete Moser approached Lancaster City Council, and found himself taking up work as a musician in residence within Lancaster City Council, Arts and Events section. Initially a one-year contract, this was soon extended to three years, funded in partnership with North West Arts Board and Lancashire County Council's Arts Unit. During those years he worked from an office at the central Arts and Events premises in Lancaster, but quickly found that much of his actual music activity was taking place in and around Morecambe, the seaside resort connected to and distinct from (it is or can be a tense relationship between the two) the historic Georgian city of Lancaster. It was a bit of a one-man-band operation then— aptly perhaps, since one of Moser's claims to performance fame was as 'the fastest one-man-band in the world'. But, in 1996, with a good track record behind him of organising community projects such as a carnival band, Moser was successful with funding applications to the National Lottery and from the Single Regeneration Budget. This led to the opening of a dedicated working space, with offices, rehearsal and recording facilities, workshop rooms, a kitchen and storerooms (for instruments and banners), called the Hothouse. It is located in a fairly run-down area of Morecambe, the West End, on the ground floor of a snooker hall premises, overlooking a square that has itself recently been renovated with a feature mosaic paving. You can't miss the Hothouse, it's brightly painted, and always busy with a buzz, sometimes boom, of activity.

2001 was another important date in the history of MMM as an organisation, for this was the year when the project formed in to a registered company with charitable status, and the year when it established the first Youth Music Action Zone in the country. There are over 24 such action zones now, funded from a significant initiative from Arts Council England to encourage music making and access to opportunities by British youth (and with a multi-million pound budget). According to Youth Music, the managing agency of the national project,

More Music in Morecambe is the lead organisation in the Lancashire Youth Music Action Zone and has built up partnerships with the local Health Authority, Youth Services, LEAs, County Arts Unit, Mid Pennine Arts, and Arts Development Officers across the county. Partnership funding will continue to come from North West Arts, Lancashire County Council and Lancaster City Council.

With levels of funding from public sources such as Youth Music, and from charitable foundations, MMM has managed to grow to include dedicated administrative staff, a small team of contracted community musicians, a pool of up to 50 freelance musicians and other specialist art workers to draw on for specific projects, a board of trustees … As the project's website explains, 'The core funding has always split between "arts" and "social" funding and the mix of these two elements allows the company to develop a wide range of work'. MMM has also built up a wide stock of equipment and instruments from numerous sources. The lottery grant allowed the company to purchase a van, a vital PA rig, lighting, computer equipment and instruments. The scope of the latter was subsequently increased by donations via the BBC's Instrument Amnesty, which supplied oboes, violins, more guitars and brass.

Moser's previous experience as a musical director for the renowned theatre and public performance company Welfare State International (founded in 1968, with a debut show/happening in Lancaster's Williamson Park) informs MMM's ideology and practice, and shows the clear strand back to some of the 1960s community arts radicalism. Earlier musical directors for Welfare State have included some leading British improvisers; the involvement in the early 1970s of pianist and composer Mike Westbrook and then maverick saxophonist Lol Coxhill, for example, provides further evidence of the links between community arts and jazz-based improvisation during these times. *Engineers of the Imagination: The Welfare State Handbook* explains the fluidity expected of the music in a Welfare State performance event:

Individual arts are continually changed and transformed. In music, for instance, you can catch the flavour of a jazzband or folkband, which have a Fifties resonance, while drawing on popular music from the start of the century or earlier. It isn't long before these are transformed—by a South American bayonne rhythm, by Celtic pipes, ska or South African Hi-Life textures, by reggae or by synthesiser. The new sounds do not replace the old ones, but colour them, and move them on into new hybrid styles.

In terms of street music, Moser's work with Welfare State led to him gaining and, characteristically, sharing experience on which instruments to choose: trumpets or cornets are 'very useful outdoors for their cutting tone, but require experienced players.... In the rain, wet lips can be a problem; bagpipes on the other hand 'create an enormous full sound [and] immediate audience response'. According to the company's founder John Fox, Welfare State sought to use:

...music that works in the street, and is not military, but has a certain kind of funky openness... It's got space within it. It's not imperialist. It allows space for the beat and it allows space for the audience. It's also theatre music, and not thought of separately from the image... As 'music' music, it has its limitations, but again, you see, it's about breaking categories.

Fox encapsulates the continuing ethos of WSI in the title of his 2002 book, *Eyes on Stalks*: for him, performance is about getting eyes on stalks, not bums on seats.

The location of MMM in the seaside town of Morecambe is emphasised in the project's alliterative name, which may give the project a certain parochial ring, that seems to gain in volume as MMM has become more ambitious in scope regionally and nationally. But what does Morecambe itself contribute? In a recent national survey based on rates of prescription of tranquillisers and anti-depressants by GPs, Morecambe came top: it was officially the most depressed town in the country; in a tongue-in-cheek alternative tourist guide book called *Crap Towns*, published in 2003, the resort was voted the third worst town in Britain. One of the book's editors,

Sam Jordison, originally from Morecambe, actually wrote its nomination document:

Poor old Morecambe. The seaside town they should never have opened. Where a silent and grey day comes as a blessed relief from the gales of black depression that generally batter its desolate promenades.
The town would be almost entirely empty if it wasn't for the fact that the DHSS have put its bed and breakfasts to good use in housing the North West's homeless and hopelessly addicted. You are now more likely to find needles on the prom than lollipop sticks.

This is unfair. Through the 1990s Morecambe benefited from massive investment, noticeably in its cultural infrastructure, with the strategy of reinventing itself as a new pleasure space. So, in came the statue to local comedian Eric Morecambe along the promenade, drawing attention to the resort's strong entertainment heritage. Summer festivals were organised each week during the season, appealing to different constituencies, generations and classes (music festivals included a prestigious annual WOMAD world music event, followed by the Holidays in the Sun punk festival). The Tern Project was a poetic public art celebration of the natural wildlife, particularly the birds, of Morecambe Bay. In important ways, then, culture was consciously employed by local politicians and investors as an engine of regeneration. Involved in this from its early days was MMM, as a creative social gesture that is now a longstanding commitment. Is there a sense of marginality working from Morecambe? As a leading music project in the North West, and one once described by the then funding organisation North West Arts as a 'jewel in its crown', one might assume that it would be located in one of the two acknowledged centres of pop music energy in the North West, Liverpool (the Beatles and Merseybeat, Institute for Popular Music, Liverpool Institute of Performing Arts, and European City of Culture 2008) or Manchester (Factory, the Hacienda, Madchester, Oasis). But *Morecambe*? There are of course strategic imperatives at work here. In a recent consultative local authority document, *A Cultural Strategy for Lancashire*, one of the critical views articulated by people across the county was that they suffered in relation to their privileged metropolitan neighbours. The proximity of the large cities was perceived as impacting negatively on the county's cultural identity, to the extent that it contributed to, as one respondent put it, 'Boundary blurring—what is Lancashire? And a sense that Manchester and Liverpool "get everything"'. Investing in Morecambe, which is on the northwest edge even of Lancashire itself, addresses such concerns. Also, MMM recognises the opportunities Morecambe offers it—and not only because its deprived and depressed state conveniently attracts grants. Morecambe is a seaside resort with excellent local expectations and traditions which MMM has sought to tap into, revive, celebrate—hence projects like the street carnival band, Baybeat, echoing northern days past with a shrill samba whistle, or the Seagull Café sing-a-longs with tea and cake for older residents of the town. In ways like this the presence of Morecambe in the project, rather than the other way round, is what intrigues. Also says Moser, 'it's a town that relies on tourism, and people need to feel good about being there, so we set out in part to make the people feel better about themselves. It's a space of fun too, and we want to contribute to that. Also it's a town of entertainers—Eric Morecambe, Thora Hird. In 2003 the hoteliers of Morecambe gave us an award for services to the entertainments industry, specifically saying that MMM has encouraged the kids in Morecambe who will in the future be some of the performers here because of the work you've all done'.

MMM projects vary from one-day sessions to five-year developments, with budgets ranging from £300 to £20,000. Unlike some other community music programmes, which emphasise the continuity of process over one-off end products, MMM projects frequently culminate in some kind of public showing, whether this is in the form of a performance, CD, booklet or poster. (In a way, the book you are reading now is one of these, too.) The work uses percussion, songwriting, poetry, creative improvisation, instrumental playing and arrangement, singing, composition, procession, costume and dance. For Moser, working to a final cultural event or performance is an important aspect of the creative process, one that fosters a sense of achievement for participants, and widens out to include the community more fully in the form of audiences (who then often invite themselves in to the performance in some way, too). MMM has worked collaboratively as well, for instance with Welfare State International, the Hallé Orchestra, Amnesty International. The range of these organisations offers a sense of the scope of the project's vision: performance and procession, classical music, social campaigning.

3

Many examples of MMM moments are found in this book. The programme of work, that has, in MMM's own words, 'touched people from cradle to grave', has included:

Baybeat Streetband
an open access band of brass players, percussionists and dancers of up to 50 people, rehearsing and performing throughout the year.

Stages
a range of work with 12-18 year olds including band work, song-making, deejaying and sound technology. This includes a monthly series of showcase gigs across Lancashire for young bands, deejays and songwriters.

Off the Rails
an old-style big band playing new-style sounds.

Safety Net
music-making sessions with a wide range of people with special needs.

Dhamak
the development of a collective of deejays, rappers and dhol drummers with Asian youth in East Lancashire.

Seagull Café
the creation of a new concert party of people aged over 55 through weekly afternoons of songs and guests, tea and cakes.

Youth Music Action Zone
lead organiser for Lancashire's activity in this high profile national initiative, and the first such zone in the country to be designated so.

Opening Times
a nationally recognised programme of training and professional development in participatory music-making in the form of weekend workshops and placements.

Conclusion

… the messiness of making (and teaching) music is an essential part of the fun.
Andrew Peggie, *Tuning Up: A New Look at Instrumental Music Teaching*

Dave Price has argued that community music has shifted 'from a movement to an industry in less than 10 years', and describes the success of this socio-cultural work as follows: 'If community music were a publicly listed company, we'd all want shares'. Price's capitalistic metaphor may provoke unease among some of the old-time radicals. They may suspect that the relatively successful trajectory of the project, with its newfound discourse and purpose of 'urban regeneration', 'creative industries', government-sponsored 'action zones', and 'educational accreditation', is evidence of its co-optation by the neo-conservative agenda. Where once SME meant the social and musical experimentation of the Spontaneous Music Ensemble, now it seems to refer to the small and medium enterprises that form a network of community music projects up and down the country. On the other hand, many view the survival and expansion of community music as the most compelling proof of its energy, legitimacy, attraction and difference. This choice between continued ideological purity, and buying into the very establishment you once sought to criticise or demolish, may anyway be a false one, encouraged by a familiar Golden Age mythology, and neither is it of course specific to community music. The growing pains of a long(er)standing community theatre ensemble like Welfare State International betray similar anxieties about community arts more generally becoming the radical establishment.

Welfare State's journey from tented alternative community in a Burnley, Lancashire quarry in the early 1970s to being housed in an award-winning, Lottery-funded, refurbished art centre in the historic Lakeland market town of Ulverston in the 1990s is too easily read as a retreat from activist endeavour into privilege and comfort, ' a long way from the trailers of 1968', as Welfare State founder John Fox puts it, with/out nostalgia. But problems and questions raised as a result of the survival and longevity of radical projects and ideas (at least from the British counterculture) are in my view relatively rare and interesting ones that we should cherish and explore—one of the aims of my own research over the years has been precisely to recover and trace such histories.

3

Far better than more dismal, familiar narratives of burnout or failure. It is emblematic that, while early Welfare State had a revolutionary 'manifesto', MMM has a corporate-style 'mission statement'—but it is more significant to consider the ways in which these voicings of intent echo each other across the decades. Its mission states that MMM exists today to 'encourage original creativity and performance', 'to create beautiful and innovative pieces of music and art' with open access for the community. These are good things to do. In this more positive interpretation, developments like community music become one of the lasting cultural, educational and social achievements of generations of idealistic cultural workers. I suspect that it is here that we should locate Pete Moser and More Music in Morecambe.

Acknowledgements

Thanks to Pete Moser (2004) and Maggie Nicols (2002) for agreeing to be interviewed. Transcriptions, and graphics, of Nicols and other interviews with British jazz and improvising musicians are available on my homepage: **www.uclan.ac.uk/facs/class/humanities/staff/mckay.htm**

RISE HIGHER

The barley field wished but swayed,
washed by rain, dried by sun
And combed by the wind

The Oak stands, centre page
I feel it stretch as morning pushes back the sheets
Her leaves twist in the breeze like confident hands
Of Indian dancers and the sun shoots through them
making shoals of golden fish swimming in her shadow...

I was looking for inspiration and there it was.
Not in the field nor the sun nor the oak,
Barely visible - NG + DA - in the trunk
I had been here before. The memory flooded back - surged
And there I was in that sea of barely seeing you.

chapter 4
Making New Music: Approaches To Group Composition
Hugh Nankivell

This chapter is about making music in groups. I shall discuss several games, exercises and approaches that have been used successfully in many different contexts with many different groups of people. In addition, I shall look at some of the most important aspects of group-music-making: its history, problems and numerous advantages. Some of the references and examples I use can be related clearly to educational use, some to Western classical composition and approaches, others to jazz, pop and world music analysis. This chapter aims to give a picture of how, why and where we might comfortably place contemporary ideas about group music-making.

4

In today's musically eclectic world there are numerous groups, ensembles and projects which are collaboratively put together and which utilise and connect musical instruments and styles from many different backgrounds. For instance, there are successful ensembles which mix Medieaval vocal polyphony with Scandinavian jazz, Dhol drum ensembles playing with bass guitar and turntable decks, punk singers working with string quartets and so on. The opportunities for cross-fertilisation and exciting collaborations are endless. This chapter does not analyse those examples, but investigates some of the potential starting points and the mental processes involved in any type of group composition. Ideas connected with give-and-take, compromise, consensus, and the thorny areas of assessment and ownership are examined. The exercises, games and pieces described below work very well with a wide range of instruments. One of the main aims of all the approaches mentioned is to encourage and develop listening skills which improve our musical skills and help us to appreciate music more. However, we need to be acutely aware of the dynamic possibilities of the instruments that we have at our disposal, especially when mixing together acoustic and amplified instruments. For instance, turntable decks are often played as a solo instrument (in clubs, for instance) and have a very rich sound world, which can dominate a group situation, if not used carefully. Similarly, an acoustic piano (especially a grand with the sustain pedal depressed) can easily overwhelm a mixed ensemble.

The material I work with is applicable to groups containing people with very different individual personal skills and experiences on their musical instruments. Much music requires a high level of individual skill before any successful ensemble playing is possible. If you want to play in a brass band, or a youth jazz orchestra or a symphony orchestra you require certain individual skills, which are then connected with others skills in an ensemble situation. However, there are ways for playing in an ensemble which are not reliant upon high individual skills or which do not rely upon 'free improvisation'. These pieces are explored below, and are particularly appropriate for mixed groups of adults and younger people who want to make music together. (In fact, several of these pieces were invented by the community band Dangerous Volume, which is a mix of parents and children working together). Of course, anyone who is playing in a band needs some skills in order to be able to integrate musically with others, but these skills are often more to do with listening and then knowing how to respond, than they are to do with a more conventional musical technique.

The exercises are described in a way which moves from the simple and straightforward to the more complex and involved as it is hoped with any ensemble, both individually and as a group, we get better the more we play, empathise with and listen to each other.

A few definitions

This chapter is called 'Making new music', and I have tried to reduce the use of too many loaded musical terms such as 'composition' or 'improvisation'. However, at times musical terms do need to be used to describe the creative process. The main drawback to the word 'composition' is that it usually refers to notated music and often to the score itself (a message from a composition teacher to a student: 'Have you handed your composition in yet?'). Also it is connected very closely to the classical Western form of music, and does not fit well with other types of music, where there is no actual notation. In a similar way, the word 'improvisation' has its drawbacks—it refers quite rightly to a music that is fleeting, that can never be tied down, but it is often used in a derogatory way (particularly when contrasted with the rather grand use of the word 'orchestrate') . Among others, Neil Sorrell has pointed out these differences, and he has used the phrases 'an orchestrated attack' as opposed to an 'improvised shelter', to highlight them. Even when it is made clear about the positive relationship between composition and improvisation (the American saxophonist Wayne Shorter says that when he's improvising he's composing very fast, and when composing he's improvising very slowly) then there are still real difficulties about using those terms, and particularly within group music-making activities. Apparently, if we are improvising then it's just messing about, and if it's composition then it's sitting on your own with a sheet of manuscript paper.

Composition is such a loaded and, for many, a difficult word, that it is worth, just briefly, looking at what it traditionally means, and then what it can mean for the future. The word composition is derived from the Latin componere, which literally means 'well put together', which in some ways is a definition of arranging. What about the idea, the germ, the start point, should that not also be a part? When the National Curriculum Music document was being put together a decade ago, there was some attempt at defining composition by stating that there were three types of composing and that these were 'improvising, composing and arranging', which in many ways only

adds to the confusion. However, we can be helped out a little by the Scottish Curriculum, which dispensed almost entirely with the word composition and replaced it with 'invention'. Yes, it's still a loaded word, but has less musical connotations and this, I believe, is a good thing. What does 'invention' mean? This word derives from the Latin *invenire* and means 'to find', the initial inspiration, the starting point, the germ of an idea. If we start with invention (finding an idea), and add it to composition (to arrange and put together), we have a workable definition for composition, which is particularly apt for group contexts where different people contribute different things towards the whole. At a very basic level if you have one person who is good at coming up with ideas and another who is good at arranging and fleshing out those ideas then you have a workable team, it's as simple as that!

There is deliberately very little musical analysis here, and none in the conventional 'score-reading' type. In most notated music, we are aware of the composer who notated it and the performers who are giving an interpretation of that 'score'. This also applies to pop/rock bands that play cover versions and to jazz big-bands who play 'classic' Ellington or Basie arrangements. However, within group music-making contexts it can sometimes be useful to be aware of who contributed what in terms of initial ideas, arrangements, improvisations, structural changes, radical alterations, dynamics, endings etc. This is a form of analysis, and the usefulness of it can be measured through the group members' understanding of their own strengths and weaknesses and subsequently their development as musicians. It is also crucially important that any attempt to examine the music that is made in this way looks (and listens) not only to the final product, but also to the process by which it was made. This music is often as much about the social interaction between people as it is about the final product. I believe that all music is ultimately about how we communicate as humans with each other, but in group-music-making we are able to witness that process of communication in a very clear way, and need to be able to respond to the process as much as to the final product.

There are examples of group-music-making that can be looked at and used as models, and it is important that this type of activity does not get pigeon-holed as a sort of 'educational- composing' as it has far more resonance than that. There are examples to be found in music from West Africa, Japan, Indonesian Gamelan, from jazz, pop and rock music, British and Irish folk music and some composers from the Western canon have also involved themselves in group music-making. However, the ideas behind group music-making are also in some ways new and exciting developments which have been stimulated and encouraged through the development of the community music movement. Some of this work and the music it produces and the discussion of the process is ground-breaking and needs to be recognised as such. Like all movements it has roots in pre-existing music, but also fuses and creates new ideas.

In addition to the many joys and revelations that emerge from being involved in group music-making there are common problems. These can be to do with individuals not getting on with each other (it happens in all groups of humans at some time or another), and there are a couple that are particularly relevant to this work. Ownership of the music can cause great distress, and in particular, whenever there is any money (or the potential for money to be) involved. Several pop/rock groups have come to grief over this issue. Normally the cause of distress has been when one member does most of the initial 'songwriting', and then other members of the group feel that their contributions (in terms of arrangement, or performance, or improvisation) are not being rewarded because they are not credited as a co-composers. Two well-known pop groups who have solved this dispute for themselves are U2 and Queen. U2 divide all their royalties up five ways, between the four members of the band and the manager. They realise that the music is the combination of all of their skills and input and, even if one person contributes more on a certain song, then it is better for the whole group if they respect that the group itself is the main thing. The band Queen nearly split up when Freddie Mercury realised that he would be getting the same amount of royalties for his song 'Bohemian Rhapsody' as would Roger Taylor (the drummer) for the song he wrote on the B-side (which of course made as many sales as the A-side!). Again, like U2 they ultimately resolved this issue happily, acknowledging that although they have different strengths they work as a group and should credit the music as being 'by Queen' for the future. When beginning to work on a group-music-project, it is therefore important to be aware that everyone involved should feel that they have

some ownership over the music, and that at times mechanisms (rules) need to be put in place in order that the group doesn't grind to a halt in deliberations or arguments.

The other thorny issue is in terms of assessment, for in many situations the music that has been created has to be assessed in some way. Teachers and examiners who have to mark music that has been created in group situations (compositions or improvisations) are faced with very testing decisions, and it can sometimes seem an impossible task. I am not going to dwell on this aspect, except to acknowledge that it is a difficult issue, and that one way around the problem is to make sure that the process through which the music has been made, is carefully documented by everyone who has been involved. This can be done by means of a diary, log-book, learning journal, recordings etc. In this way not only does the 'assessor' get a bigger picture of what has happened, but it also gives all the participants a way of detailing their contributions and it informs them as to their strengths and potential weaknesses for future group music-making projects.

'Playing' music: five ideas, games and exercises

One way that I begin workshops or projects is by explaining that we are all going to be 'playing' music. Play is a very important word and I think some people, especially those who have been making music for years and years, forget that the verb used to describe what we do with music is, most commonly, play. If we are comfortable with the idea of 'playing music' then we should not be at all worried about playing games or trying out exercises. Some musicians seem to think that games (and this word relates closely to 'play') are for children and not for when we have studied music and can already 'do it'. We can all benefit from warming up, from having fun with music and from playing games that, at the very least for instance, develop our listening skills.

Many of the starting points I use are concerned with playing rhythmically together. By this means, not only can I begin to relate musicians of different skill levels together (in a way that would not be possible if I began by talking about pitches or harmony, for instance) but also I can easily relate the musical exercises and games we are doing to pre-existing musical traditions. Samba, Steel pans and Gamelan music are all ensemble-musics that can be taught (at a rudimentary level) very quickly

to a group of mixed abilities who can benefit and enjoy playing to quite a high standard in a short time. All of the games and exercises can be expanded, developed and extended. When engaged on composition or songwriting projects I often point out that all music sounds a bit like some other music and that there are very few original ideas in the world, but that it is what you do with an idea that makes it interesting, original, useful, fun, enjoyable. So if you like the following games and exercises, then take them, develop them, make them your own and have fun playing them.

Name Game

I will normally begin working with a group by using a simple name game. For this game you need to be in a circle, standing or sitting. Begin by clapping a simple rhythm, that has got a gap in it somewhere. Loop the rhythm, repeating it over and over, and ask the group to listen to what you are doing until they feel comfortable to join in. Once everyone has joined in, and you are happy that everyone has learned the rhythm then stop clapping and ask everyone else to stop.

Next explain that you will develop this into a call and response game. You will all begin the rhythm again, and in the first gap you are going to say your name (nice and clearly), in the next gap everybody else is going to echo your name. In the next gap, the person on your left (or right) is going to say their name (alone, as a solo) and in the fourth gap everyone repeats that name. This process continues with the next person (solo first time, everyone the second) all the way around the circle.

What are the reasons for playing such a game ? First, it lets you, the workshop leader, know if the group has understood your instructions and whether they can play a rhythm together. If they cannot achieve this, then it should be clear that the group will need to do some other straightforward exercises, before developing. However, if they are able to play the game successfully, all around the circle, then this demonstrates that, as a group, they have a mutual rhythmic competence. Second, if successfully played, it also shows that they understand the difference between solo and group (ensemble), that they are prepared to perform (clapping and using their voice) and that their listening and performing skills are developed enough for them to be able to take on more musically interesting tasks. Third, everyone in the group can learn quite a lot about each other from playing this game. For instance who are the loud

4

and who are the quiet people, who gets obviously nervous before performing their 'solo' (name), who is smiling as they play and who is frowning. This learning can be very useful for when more interesting and complex games and pieces are later played.

Some tips for the 'Name Game':

1 It helps if the rhythm that you begin to clap at the outset is not too fast or too complicated. A rhythm in 4 is a good start and the simplest one might be to clap three beats and then leave the gap as the fourth beat. If it is clear that the group can cope with a simple rhythm then maybe later try a more demanding one, but it is always better to start off easy and get more difficult rather than put off people by attempting something that is (or seems to be) beyond them and then having to backtrack to a simpler starting point.

2 When you start this game remember that some names are considerably longer than others (Elizabeth is 4 times longer than Zac and if you are in a class some teachers might feel compelled to say the name the class normally knows them as—for instance, Mrs O'Sullivan, which is half as long again).

3 This game can go on for a long time if you have a big group (25 and over). This is fine, but people may get tired, hands ache and some of the group may be bored.

Playing a game as simple as the 'Name Game' enables musical terminology to be used and introduced. Words such as 'solo' 'tutti' 'ostinato', 'rest' and many more can be mentioned and described. Quite often when I play this game I try to find ten words that mean the same as 'rest' or 'pause', soon after introducing the game. This is good if we are moving on to writing songs later. Also, when discussing the game afterwards it can be a very good listening exercise to ask how many people heard names with three or four syllables in, and what difference the syllable length made to the ease with which people could put their names into the gap. It can also be worth discussing, as a group, how nervous individuals felt when it was their turn to do their solo, and to mention how this compares with performance nerves. Asking the group if anyone made a mistake can also be a valuable question, especially if you emphasize that it does not matter that you made a mistake (providing you did not do it on purpose) but that it is important that we learn from our mistakes.

The 'Name Game' has many possible developments, but I will just mention one that I often play. Everyone claps the rhythm as in the first version and in the first gap (break, hole, pause rest…) I start, but instead of saying my own name, I say the name of somebody else in the circle. In the next gap that person has to say the name of somebody else and so on. This is very good for responding to each other, to being aware of which people respond well and which people are a bit slower. So playing the 'Name Game' has many more benefits than the very important one of learning the names of the group that you are working with.

'Musical Tennis' is another moderately simple game, but is a step-up from the 'Name Game'. It is a game that, to start with, simply uses claps and finger-clicking, but it can develop onto instruments or voices, or it can become part of a bigger piece of music, and it can have additional rules. When you begin to play 'Musical Tennis', it is quite mechanical (with strict and clear counting) but it can become much more musical and spontaneous after the group has internalised the rules and the process. I learned this game from a guitarist in London called Adrian Lee. He composes and performs music for theatre. We played together in a palindromically-named improvising band called Was It A Car Or A Cat I Saw, and we often used this exercise as a warm-up. I have subsequently used it in primary schools, with instrumentalists from Opera North and the Royal Opera House, with students doing a music degree and with drummers on a percussion weekend.

Musical Tennis

This is a game for pairs, which develops listening and responding to each other. All the sounds that are played are on the beat, there is no irregular playing, or syncopation or off-beats. Everything comes in four-beat packages. (Or, if you prefer, four beats to the bar.)

Player One begins and s/he can clap one or two times and then must click. In the tennis analogy Player One is serving and the click is the ball going over the net. Depending on how many beats are left (out of the four), Player Two fills those in by clapping those.

You could think of it like this:

~ * / # ~ * * / # ~ * * / # # ~ * / etc

key:
Player One clap = # and click = ~
Player Two clap =* and click = +
/ = marking the end of the 4-beat package

All through the above example Player One is serving.
However, if Player One does a click on the fourth beat of the bar—for instance, # # # ~ / —then this passes over the serving (or 'leading' in musical terms) to Player Two, who immediately continues without losing or missing a beat.

Here is an example where the serving changes twice:

~ * / # ~ * * / # ~ * * / # # ~ * /# # # ~/ * * + # / * + # # / * * * + / # # ~ */ etc

When written down like this it can appear quite complicated, but persevere, because it will become very rewarding. Some tips:

1 It is important to keep the beat steady at all times. If you are playing this in a room with several pairs at the same time, then it can be useful to have someone keeping the beat on an instrument (a cowbell or woodblock, for instance).

2 When playing this game you might discover (especially if you are playing it in a room with other pairs) that you are listening to each other with your eyes more than with your ears. It is important to be aware that in music-making lots of communication and listening is done through eye contact rather than listening.

3 Player One does not have to clap at all, but can begin with a click, this really keeps his/her partner on their toes.

4 If someone says (as they often do) that they cannot click their fingers then there are two very positive responses. Firstly, explain that this is a good opportunity for them to learn how to click their fingers, as it is only through trying that they will learn. Secondly, if they are finding it too hard, then use a different sound, such as tapping the chest, slapping thighs.

5 When playing in a group it can be a good rule to say that once the game has started no-one is allowed to speak. If one pair's game breaks down, then someone must just start it again without discussing it!

'Musical Tennis' has a number of benefits. It develops very good communication between two players: it usually requires eye contact, and it needs both musicians to be aware of each other and to be ready to respond. Also, it is a game at which neither player can 'win', but they both can succeed (by keeping a long 'rally' going) or they both fail (if the 'rally' collapses after the first serve). From the workshop leader's perspective, you can learn lots about the group from playing this game, especially regarding who has and who lacks confidence and who is prepared to volunteer themselves as a guinea-pig/soloist. (When you have explained the game, you normally need a volunteer to try it out, so that those who may not have understood the explanation can see it demonstrated in practice.) There are many wonderful journeys that this game can be taken on and developed into. Putting it onto instruments is one, having different pairs conducted in and out is another, expanding the four-beat rule to either four or eight beats is another and so on. The game seems endless in possible developments and musical fun.

'Goat Music' is a piece which has a simple structure (ABA) and works very well in many different contexts. It was devised by Dangerous Volume, a community music group based in Huddersfield, and has now been performed by other community bands, school-groups and student ensembles. Dangerous Volume players range from those who have highly developed musical skills and are musically confident, to those who are musically inexperienced and unconfident. Before inventing 'Goat Music' as a structure, we had been working on rhythmically playing together, especially in terms of one person setting up a riff on top of which others would join in. We were getting very comfortable, confident and musical in the way that we could build up these overlapping ostinati and so began to make 'pieces' using this approach. We also invented a piece we called 'Bump Gong Chinese Cow' which was similar to 'Goat Music' but had more fiddly parts and required particular instruments. 'Goat Music' is simple enough, but also broad enough, to have remained popular over the years since it was invented.

4

In 'Goat Music', everyone has to play two instruments, these being a pitched instrument and an unpitched one. One person could sing and clap, another could play violin and drum, a third could play xylophone and cowbell, for example. As long as the group is able to play rhythmically together, it does not really matter what experience different people have on their instruments, and we have found that often the best pieces are made when there is a mix of people with highly developed instrumental skills playing alongside novices. This piece has been played by small groups (five or six players) and with large groups (20 plus), but we have found that 5-12 is ideal.

Goat Music

Part One. The piece begins with one person playing an ostinato on their pitched instrument. Gradually everyone else joins in playing their own riff, but one that locks into the first riff (and anyone else who may have subsequently joined it). Once everyone has joined in on their pitched instrument, one person decides to change to their unpitched instrument, and so (with a short rest or not) begins a different ostinato, but in the same overall groove. This is the signal for everyone else gradually to make the shift from their pitched instruments to their unpitched instrument.

Part Two. Once everyone is playing their unpitched instrument (and this section is often, understandably, louder then the first section) one person decides to move back to their pitched instrument and begins a third ostinato, again within the same overall rhythmic feel. At this point everyone else one-by-one moves back to their pitched instruments.

Part Three. Once everyone is playing the pitched instruments again, one person decides to stop playing. Gradually everybody stops playing, until there is only one left. Then s/he stops too.

Finally, as a group you discuss what type of goat that music represented. It is important to remember that there are no right or wrong answers, just ideas, and feelings.

Some observations based on my experience of playing 'Goat Music' with people.

• Before introducing it make sure that the group is comfortable with what a riff/ostinato is and that everyone can play together. Try to discourage riffs that are too busy. This is for two main reasons: so that you do not get too tired (especially wind players), but probably more importantly so that not all the musical space is filled. Riffs played by solo electric guitarists in rock bands are not generally good models for 'Goat Music'.

• Versions of 'Goat Music' where limited pitches are predetermined often work really well. This is especially the case when you have a mixture of tuned percussion (eg xylophones with only the white notes) with other tuned instruments. In this situation it can be worth suggesting using just five notes (a pentatonic scale) to begin with.

• Think about how you sit or stand in relation to each other. It is good in this piece if everyone can have eye-contact with each other, and so a circle is good. If you regularly rehearse in a circle, do remember though that performing in a circle is not good for an audience.

• 'Goat Music' can work with some pre-decisions, for instance you could decide which person starts each section and who ends the piece or you could have a conductor/leader making these decisions as the piece flows.

• It might well be worth practising endings, as in many groups there is someone who always wants to be the person who ends the piece, and this might not always be to everyone's liking. (In Dangerous Volume there is a 10-year old drummer called Joel who always likes to be the last to play in 'Goat Music'!)

While Dangerous Volume have used this piece as a performing piece, another community band, Off The Rails, based in Morecambe and led by Ben McCabe, have found the piece valuable as a warm-up piece, and have regularly used it at the beginning of rehearsals. I have used it with primary school groups, and find that it is a great piece for using multiple tuned percussion (xylophones, glockenspiels, metallophones, chime bars) and recorders. It is also a good exercise which can also be treated as a performance piece. The fact that individuals always have ownership of their own parts is one of its really exciting and original aspects.'

4

A piece I call 'Conducted 12345' is an extremely rewarding way of playing structured music in a group, where there are five basic rules, a conductor, and endless possibilities. While it is simple to understand, it does rely upon some understanding and internalising of musical terminology. However, it does not require the players to understand the terminology before you embark on the piece, and so it is often an educational journey as well as a purely musical one. I learned this piece from a London-based composer called Paul Griffiths, a guitarist, performer and composer who works extensively with students at the Guildhall School of Music. One of the great things about working with Griffiths, especially with teenagers and younger musicians is that, in addition to his genuine inspiration and motivation as a player and workshop leader, he never uses or mentions conventional five-staff notation. He can make and inspire wonderfully organic music which involves everyone as a creative participant.

Conducted 12345

requires a conductor and a group of musicians (I have played this piece in groups ranging from five to about 50). The conductor will use hand signals addressed (initially) to each individual in turn to indicate when and what to play and when to stop. To start, the conductor holds up 1,2, 3, 4 or 5 fingers up while looking at an individual player and to stop the conductor (again while making eye contact with that player) closes his/her hand into a fist. If the conductor holds one finger up, then this indicates that the player must play a drone. Two fingers means an ostinato, three fingers a gentle solo, four fingers a different more angular solo and five fingers means to use the voice. As this indicates, it is necessary for the group to understand what all these terms mean, but these can be explained in a creative and practical way through actually playing. In my experience, this is a great way of explaining terms, including drone, ostinato, staccato and legato. It is also a good way of exploring other similes for the musical terms, which might well mean more to some people. Here are some examples:

1   drone, single note, long, sustained

2   ostinato, riff, loop, repeated pattern

3   solo (a) flowing, legato, stepwise, smooth

4   solo (b) angular, staccato, aggressive, big interval leaps

5   voice (to possibly include singing, speaking, whispering, chanting, shouting, humming).

When trying out all of the rules of 'Conducted 12345' it is worth discussing and exploring what each rule means, or could mean, on each instrument. For instance, playing a drone on a sustaining instrument such as a flute or a violin or a keyboard is fairly straightforward, but what do instruments that do not have much sustaining power, such as a guitar, piano or many percussion instruments do? Some other observations from experience:

- It can often be good to begin this piece by having only the first three rules, and then to develop it from there, whereby rule three is simply 'solo'. Once the group is comfortable with these three rules, then the others (and indeed more) can be added.

- It is good to play 'Conducted 12345' after you have played 'Goat Music' (or similar) because of the need in Goat Music to work on the idea of ensemble groove and ostinato playing. In this piece it is essential that if someone is given the number 2 signal (ostinato) that they keep it steady and consistent, and that if any other players are also asked to play 2, then they lock in with the first player (just like in 'Goat Music'). I have found it useful when playing 'Conducted 12345' to rehearse playing with only rule 2 (just adding and deleting players) for quite a while.

- If you play this piece with a group over a series of sessions, or if you know the group very well, then it will become apparent which players are especially interesting when soloing, or who can keep very steady grooves, or who always plays loud etc. This piece is a great one for really developing and discussing these elements of ensemble playing and listening and also discussing with players their own perceived strengths and weaknesses.

- This piece is very flexible, and can have certain sections predetermined. When I first worked on this piece with Griffiths, we were spending two days together exploring ideas of personal musical development with a group of players from the Hallé Orchestra. During those two days, we tried a whole range of different exercises out with these very able, but sometimes quite nervous, musicians. Griffiths spent one session with two percussionists and they developed a really interesting semi-salsa groove. He said to them at one point that he would like to incorporate it into the big piece (as it turned out it was the 'Conducted 12345' piece, although I didn't know it at the time) that we would be working on later. He had a special signal for this rhythm, and it gave a different shape to the whole piece, through incorporating something already known into the unknown structure.

4

- Similarly new rules can be added. On another occasion, when I played this piece on an MMM weekend course on 'making new music', we added a rule 6, which on that occasion was 'Country and Western'. As you can imagine, this gave the piece a very different flavour.

There are many other potential extensions to this piece, from the very simple, including of dynamics into the equation, to the slightly more complex of getting a group of musicians to all start one section (a drone or a solo for instance) at the same time. An undergraduate music-student, Laura, who recently attended an MMM 'Ways Into Workshops' weekend took the basic idea of this piece and concocted her own version just for voices, with rules 1 and 2 the same, but rule 3 being duet conversations between members of the group. In this arrangement there was no conductor, so the group could freely change, move, stop and listen. It worked really well and was very enjoyable to sing.

'Conducted 12345' is a structure that works really well with a mixed ability group. It may be that some players only feel comfortable with one, or two rules for instance, but that is fine and the piece will still work. Additionally, you can then discuss how in other ensemble music (orchestras, brass bands, gamelans, choirs, rock bands etc) there is a clear understanding that different players have different roles from each other, and some are more prominent than others, but that the whole only works because of all the constituent components. It is important to share the conducting around, and (ideally) to give everyone who wants to, a chance to conduct the group. This is, for many, a liberating experience, for it gives a sense of power, surprise, enjoyment, worry and thrill all at the same time.

Other 'conducted' pieces can be used at either a more rudimentary level than 'Conducted 12345' or at a more complex and i n v o l v e d level. When working with younger children I have frequently used ideas of conducting, but without a score as a starting point for making music. I explain that the children can all invent their own musical sound (voices, bodies, instruments…) and—to begin with—I conduct them, with simple symbols for starting and stopping. (These can be easily developed with additions of dynamics, or pitch change if the group understands and responds well to the initial starting point.) If I begin as the conductor, then I am the arranger of the music, by choosing and selecting which sounds should come where and for

how long, for instance, and the performing group are the inventors of the sounds. In this way, we quickly and collaboratively make new music, and it is easy with this basic premise to get a member of the group to become the conductor and for you to become one of the 'orchestra'. At the other end of the spectrum there are musicians who have developed highly complex versions of conducting, whereby the performers do not have any notated music, but they learn (a bit like the 'Conducted12345' rules) a moderately complex set of rules for interpreting in their own way. An American musician, Butch Morris, has developed this method of group music-making and has termed it 'conduction'. He has made many wonderful pieces of music with musicians from many different backgrounds, including folk, jazz, classical, non-Western and improvisers.

I played for several years with a string quartet called 'Lapis'. We played improvised music, and invented many exercises and approaches to group playing. The piece we called 'Six Chords' works very well with groups of similar sustaining instruments (eg a group of wind players or a group of bowed string players). It does differ significantly from the four examples already detailed. It is less good for mixed instruments or instruments that do not sustain, for instance. It is good for groups of three to six players and it requires the instrumentalists to be able to play in tune and to listen very well. Further, it is not reliant upon the group playing rhythmically tightly together.

Six Chords

The rules are very simple. Before playing, each person decides upon the six notes they are going to play, without discussing these with anyone else. One of the players will then lead the playing and the six chords are played (one note per bow, or per breath, so quite slowly). After the six chords are played, they are repeated at the same speed a few more times so that the players get used to the sounds of the chords, the intonation, the chords that are more clashing, the chords that are more resolved etc. After playing the sequence several times (say, five to eight), the players gradually depart from the chords and improvise, but in a way that relates to the sound world of those chords, which will usually be quite slowly and with careful listening to each other. At some point during the improvising section, the players return to the six chords, and after playing them a couple of times the piece finishes.

4

I have used 'Six Chords' in several situations (including on MMM courses) and, while some performances are better than others, the piece always reveals several things.

- There are normally good debates about which of the chords was more consonant and which more dissonant and which players liked which chords.

- In discussions afterwards, it is frequently noted that to begin with several players do not like the sounds of the chords, but as they are repeated over and over, get to understand them more and to like them and to understand their function (in increasing tension or a release of that tension).

- All the players have equal ownership of the piece, and it is truly a collaborative experience. Whilst the idea for the piece itself exists (Lapis 'invented' it if you like) the actual content is entirely created by the group of performers.

- Finally, there is often a desire to notate the chords afterwards, or to work out some other way of remembering the sequence. 'Six Chords' can in this way lead on to other compositions or developments at further rehearsals or performances.

A few other ideas and remarks, briefly

There are many other pieces and games that I use regularly in group music-making. These have been found, borrowed, adapted, nicked, devised, invented, collaborated upon. Do remember that there are many other musicians who actively work in this area and who have very different approaches to collaboratively generating new material. I will just mention two whose ways of working I have witnessed, as they significantly differ from the approaches given above. First, Nick Hayes is a community musician (composer and performer) who currently works extensively for the Irene Taylor Trust on prison music projects. He has a wonderful approach to making music in groups which is highly organic in that he will get somebody to start off playing (probably rhythmically) and then will not stop the piece at all for sometimes upwards of half an hour. He will encourage different

members to add other parts, call out instructions and ask for ideas all while the piece is still going. This has the effect of being really exciting and stimulating and produces music that is different from that which is made in a stop-start way.

Second, Makoto Nomura is a Japanese musician who works with mixed ensembles of children and adults in devising and composing new pieces. He has invented a system of composition called 'Shogi Composition'. The piece begins by making up a 'score'. Each person writes the first part of a piece of music at the top of the page (this could be an instruction, a picture, a segment of five-staff notation…). S/he then passes the paper on to the next person who adds a further element to the piece, and so on. This is quite like the game of 'consequences'. Once the 'score' has been made then the piece is played. This approach works really well with mixed ensembles, it gives all the members of the group an opportunity to express themselves, and it leads to very good discussions about the value, importance and variety of notation.

In conclusion, the music discussed and the ideas explored in this chapter can be appreciated in many different contexts, and I hope that you will find some use from them. I believe that, as I said in the introduction, it is important that group music-making does not become pigeon-holed as a kind of music only done in educational contexts, or only as a set of exercises that can lead on to other more 'valuable' ways of making music. I do also believe that it is important to make space at the end of pieces for discussion of the creative process of music-making, whether it takes the form of 'What sort of "goat" was that?' or 'Which was the most discordant section and shall we notate it?' It is very difficult to examine this music using traditional analytical tools and so it is important we find new ways to appreciate it in terms of the social, developmental and musical skills that it can encourage and promote, and that we are able to be aware of how important the process is, as opposed to the product, and the context within which we listen to it.

4

Acknowledgements

Thanks to the many people and groups who have shaped and influenced this chapter, especially the community band Dangerous Volume, the Lapis String Quartet, the improvising ensemble Was It A Car Or A Cat I Saw (and the guitarist Adrian Lee from that band). Also, Huddersfield University for allowing me to teach and explore these techniques and approaches with undergraduate students, Lydgate Special School, Paul Griffiths, Laura Taylor, Nick Hayes, and Makoto Nomura.

DON'T MISS YOUR CONNECTION

Either disconnected engaged or getting through
It's a busy line there's no time. There's lists of things to do.
Many say that art is lazy, illegitimate and artists suspect.
While many are busy getting through, art only connects.

No money, no girlfriend, no job ... but I'm in a band.

Seen on a t-shirt in Liverpool

chapter 5
bandwork

by Martin Milner

Bands are a vital part of our culture, and, among young people in particular, they constitute one of the most persistent contemporary models of music-making. Bands enable people to support each other's creative invention and they validate the artistic process. They provide a context in which the music is 'real', and on the terms set by the musicians themselves. A band is of course a group of people playing music together, working with a group dynamic to create music. As such, many of the tools and approaches discussed elsewhere in this book apply when working with bands. The difference in this chapter is a focus on bands that come ready-formed to a community music project, or bands that form naturally within one. What follows is a discussion of 'bandwork', with practical exercises and tips for music facilitators working with bands, informed and illustrated by personal experience. In short, a framework and a toolkit.

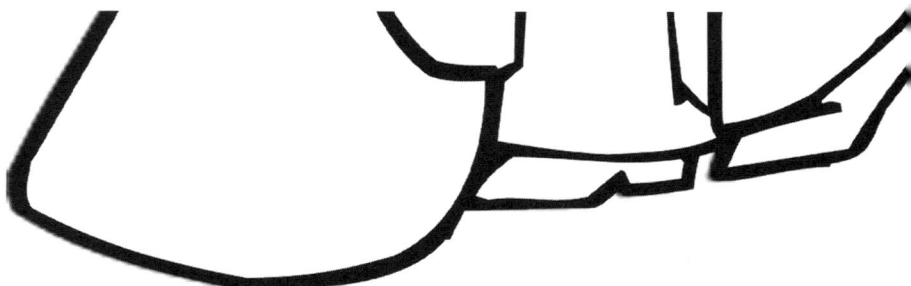

5

In my working life as a community musician, a music teacher and a project manager for youth music projects, I have gathered experience of many bands, as a member and otherwise. Very few of them have achieved global commercial success, but most (I like to think all) of them have produced meaningful music. I conclude with what I have called 'my personal bandwagon', which is effectively a short résumé of some of the various bands I have been in over the decades—not for reasons of ego, but because I found it an informative and illuminating exercise to produce. It revealed or confirmed for me the motivations and rewards I personally have experienced through the group music-making activity that is being in a band. This has also influenced my approach to the educational or community side of music-making that is bandwork.

To illustrate the kind of context that is present when doing bandwork, consider a small number of musicians (typically from three to seven) who between them devise songs (words and music) and develop a group sound that is identifiably their own, in whatever style or genre they choose. One characteristic of bands is the importance of the vocalist(s), whether a rapper, MC or singer, and by implication the importance of the lyrics—or 'message'—of the band. This model is not the only one, or even necessarily the best. (In 2004, the White Stripes were successful with only two people playing between them drums, electric guitar and voice. At the other end of the spectrum, the Polyphonic Spree and collectives like So Solid Crew had at least a dozen members.) Anyone doing bandwork should try to keep his or her mind open to all the possibilities. Tribute bands aside, it would be a mistake to attempt to shoehorn groups of musicians into a replica of another band. Every group of individuals has the capacity to create an ensemble that is in some way unique to them, and with this way of thinking it should be possible to create a band of some sort from whatever number of people playing whatever combination of instruments available. Music is made by people with instruments. Any people, any instruments.

As far as my own approach to bandwork goes, musical style is not the most important factor. Whatever gender, ethnicity or culture the musicians come from, bandwork is about enabling that group to explore their own creativity on their own terms. It is therefore beyond style. It is about working with the group's dynamic—the personalities and abilities of the members—and helping them learn the skills and

generate the confidence to develop a group sound that works for them. If the group members get to know each other, get on well, understand each other's motivations and characteristics, the style of music will largely sort itself out. When you get it right, everyone knows, because suddenly the music flows, and each member feels like an integral part of the overall sound. In fact, it is at this social level that the community musician or facilitator can usefully intervene, as much as at a musical level.

Stars in their eyes, stars in their community

There is an element to bandwork that must deal with the motives of the musicians who attend the workshops. Many young people hope to gain fame and fortune by their music, and so perhaps will aim to sound commercial (or what they think might be commercial), referencing current trends as heard on the radio or seen on television. The community musician cannot guarantee such commercial success: he or she can help the band achieve musical results, and should be clear about this. These might include, for example, stronger vocals, tighter rhythmic playing, more interesting arrangements or the use of unusual instruments or effects. It is also the case that those who run bandwork sessions must negotiate at some level their position in relation to the dream factory of pop and rock success. Do we risk encouraging young musicians to enter an industry that seems to promise so much—fame, fortune, glamour—but actually delivers its riches to a tiny proportion of those who start out into it? Are we complicit, even at grassroots level, in sustaining the trend towards global and trans-national control of the industry in which bands exist? A further symptom of this cultural power is a strong demand to perform cover versions of hit songs, which the participants may well know inside out—including all the subtleties of studio production techniques. The community musician has to decide whether or not to pursue this route in the workshops. The chances of it sounding 'good'—that is, like the original—are generally low. Would it be better to compose something similar that the participants can have ownership of, which no-one can compare to a well-known hit?

A more experienced musician might suggest other measures of success and other ways of sustaining a band than the obvious commercial record deal route. Being a popular and acclaimed band in your home town or region, with enough paid gigs to sustain r e h e a r s a l s , recordings and expenses, can offer an extremely satisfying reward: it gives the musicians (and the community) a sense of identity, of purpose, and justifies the whole activity. There is a need for good bands at the community level as well as the global one—perhaps more so, as local bands are more accessible to audiences, more connected. I try to encourage workshop attendees to think about the role of musicians historically, and globally, as minstrels, story-tellers, griots, almost 'public servants' expected to play for weddings, births, deaths, coming of age rituals and all sorts of other occasions. While this is perhaps not the first goal a young band would aim for, it remains a valid one, and draws the focus towards vital (but non-commercial) roles for the musicians in their community.

Questions of bandwork

Forming
Storming
Norm-ing
Performing
Mourning and Re-forming ...

For bands to be successful in terms of creativity and longevity (and therefore possibly commercially) the individual members must be able to get on with each other. This results in a group dynamic that inevitably becomes the identity of the band. Any community musician who takes on a band for a series of workshops must therefore consider what is going on: whether one member is acknowledged as the main originator of the music, how the others contribute, who (if anyone) takes on organisational or management-type roles, and what each member gets (or stands to get) from these arrangements. Depending on how long the band members have been together, this dynamic will be more or less established. It might be that it is working well, the band producing lots of material that everyone is happy with and that is—perhaps more importantly?—successful with audiences. It is just as possible, however, that the dynamic has settled into a comfortable but not very inspired groove, which is not challenging or rewarding some or all of the band members. The community musician must decide if and how to intervene. If the intended outcome is to help each individual band member get more, musically, out of the situation, or to help the band through a 'sticky patch', intervention will have to be considered, if only tacitly.

What is involved in being in a band? Forming, developing and, in particular, sustaining a band are some of the hardest things I have ever done. In the early stages of a band's career (before you can afford roadies) the scenario might go something like this:

choosing a name, an image, an approach

investing in rehearsal rooms, gear, transport, recording demos etc;

lifting and shifting the gear

hustling for gigs and dealing with managers and agents

travelling to strange places for gigs

waiting: for sound-check, waiting before the gig, waiting to get paid afterwards so you can get your gear and go home; etc.

buzzing on the energy and adrenaline of the gig itself

enjoying the nice period immediately after as much as possible

arguing about roles, sounds, songs, goals and of course, Forming, Storming, Norm-ing, Performing, Mourning and Re-forming ...

What does the band hope to achieve? Thinking back to when I started out in my first serious band, as an idealistic 19-year old, I tried to recall what we wanted to achieve. Was it nothing less than world domination and triple platinum albums, wealth and international jet-setting? Or changing the world with our positive message about love and life and internationalism? Or just recognition? What did we settle for? At what point did we realise that the bigger prizes were not going to be ours? Were we suffering from illusions about the perilous nature of The Business? I think the truth was this: I was in a band mostly because I was a musician, and that's what we musicians do: we make music. I did have ideals, and I certainly wanted to avoid boring dead-end jobs or the greed-fuelled business options that seemed to pervade British society during the Thatcher years. Sometimes I performed on my own, but I enjoyed being part of a band for all the weight and power of five or six people playing together, and for the camaraderie that went along with it. For musicians, the act of playing music requires no other justification—it is its own reward. So I joined or formed bands in order to play music, and not necessarily to achieve fame and fortune. To earn enough to keep going was the bottom line, and to present a certain philosophy of life (one might even say political stance) was important too. I respected and admired bands that challenged predominant social attitudes, or sang about life in ways that seemed more real than what the general media was presenting, and I wanted to be part of that too. I didn't want to be a 'pop star' like Kylie or Robbie. I was more influenced by Sixties and Seventies groups and the way they seemed to be a vital part of their culture. More recently, with Pop Idol mania and obsession with celebrity for its own sake, there are new reasons for wanting to make music. However, the older ones still exist: fame and fortune might be part of the motivation, but they are not enough without a deeper commitment to creativity, art and culture. And of course, as I point out in workshops, there are quicker and easier ways to make money than being in a band!

Set an exercise in which the band is encouraged to establish some goals. Some must be realistic and achievable in the near future, in order to generate sense of progress.

Short-term examples could include: a three song demo recording, artwork for publicity, or a strong set of 10 songs ready to gig.

Medium-term examples could be: a regional or UK tour within two years; self-produced CD album for direct sale within two years;

Longer term 'Big Dreams and Grand Schemes', along the lines of: what famous bands or musicians we will have on our European tour; who we would like to guest on our next album; what we will do with our millions from the third platinum album; what causes or charities we would consider supporting, etc.

How can a band progress, commercially and artistically? The obvious progression route—and the hope of most teenagers who set out to be pop stars—is fame and fortune. However, most bands w i l l never achieve the heights of commercial success that they seek. (No reason not to try, of course, but it is important to bear in mind and be clear about routes and probabilities. What kind of fame and fortune do they want? Do they really want it—are they hungry enough? Are there any circumstances in which they would not want it, such as certain sacrifices they might have to make?) One important outcome will be peer recognition and audience acclaim. This can be as simple as regular gigs played locally, which are well attended. Another aim— and the key one as far as I am concerned—is the artistic one: the creation of good, beautiful, maybe even challenging, music. This route may, at times, be at odds with both the former goals. However, it is a valid one, and the workshop leader could do well to remind the group of it from time to time, especially when they are not achieving what they want in terms of fame, fortune or recognition.

Oh yeah: music is an art form, isn't it! Let's make good music!

Suggest drawing up a band agreement, even if there's not a royalty in sight. Use the Musicians' Union templates as a starting point. I try to have some copies of these with me. Some press cuttings of famous court cases (the Beatles or Oasis, for instance) about bands' lawyers arguing over royalties can be illuminating—or mention the problems Jimi Hendrix had trying to extricate himself from a record company contract he once signed for $1, before he was experienced.

Sounds like teen spirit
the group dynamic of line-up, repertoire, rehearsal

What is the chemistry between the members of the band? What is the group dynamic of the band? Who writes the songs, and how do the other members fit in? Has the band tried different combinations of lyric-writers and music-writers? Have they tried jamming from cold to make new material? Who decides what the overall sound might be? These do need discussing, because there are fundamental practical considerations at stake here. What kind of friendships and rivalries exist? Will the band split everything equally—like the Rolling Stones or U2—and stay together, or will someone claim (perhaps legitimately) to deserve more than the others and drive that wedge that splits the

band? These are worth discussing in bandwork, with the music facilitator acting as mediator and prompt, posing useful questions and offering his or her own experience and advice. One issue that should inevitably arise is that of intellectual property rights and ownership of the songs and recordings.

It is important to consider the typical band culture in terms of gender, where girls sing and dance, and boys play guitars and drums. Sometimes it is so deeply ingrained among young people that they do not even think about it. (Early teens can be wary of the opposite sex, and tend to pigeonhole each other.) Peer pressure can make it hard for a young person to summon the courage to be different. This is where a sensitive community musician can offer support and encouragement, and point to appropriate role models. Certainly for young women it is less likely that they will be invited (or want) to join a band of teenage boys. If they want to get a piece of the action, perhaps the best route (at least temporarily) is to form or join a female-only band. In fact, Mavis Bayton in *Frock Rock: Women Performing Popular Music* in music production and education, has argued forcefully for 'the strategic effectiveness of separatism as a temporary p o l i t i c a l strategy for increasing the number of young women musicians'. This can work the other way, too: part of the attraction of being in a band for young men is that it can offer a way to relate with other men in a positive way—something that can be difficult without a formal structure and shared purpose. So I would never force the issue, but I would offer support for people to try things they haven't done before, or to do things in different ways. It is not and should not be just a boy thing, but sometimes we need to recognise as well that bandwork is a creative space for young men to work through their socialisation.

In terms of repertoire, making their own songs or doing cover versions is a basic choice for bands. Most opt to write their own stuff, but a few well-chosen covers can reflect a band's influences and help define its style. It is also a way of learning more about how songs are constructed, and about sharpening the band member's critical ear: with a cover it is relatively straightforward to judge when it sounds 'right', because the original is there to compare it with.

> At some stage in a project I invite the band to compare their sound to others. The music worker may have a wider knowledge, and what seems original to the band may sound familiar to him or her. Does it matter? Does the band have something to say beyond style? Does the band have a unique sound? Perhaps there is an unusual combination of instruments, or they are played in a special way. Think about successful bands you like and what makes their sound. Your choice of cover versions (if any) can lead to long discussions that shed light on people's influences and inspirations. Being able to disagree is important here.

Try to avoid obvious gimmicks while developing a particular s o u n d , both individually and as a group. Singers might use a microphone with a particular effect (reverb, EQ, and so on); drummers might use extra 'toys' such as wood-blocks, bells, midi-trigger pads to set off samples etc. Guitarists and bassists are spoiled for choice with effects units, but can easily sound just like the factory pre-sets. Work on a small number of sounds and stick to them.

If you are in a band you have to perform. You have to do gigs and you have to record, otherwise there really is no point. This is an obvious place where the experienced community musician can help, with contacts and advice. A lot of youth music work now includes getting bands to the point where they can make a decent demo recording and perform at a showcase-style gig. In most cases these will be 'first time experiences' for the bands. To get to that stage requires rehearsals. A rehearsal is a social and an artistic event. Sometimes it is more important to, for example, cheer up the bass-player after a spilt with her boyfriend, than to nail that new song. Having said that, especially when time is limited (and expensive) it is good to be highly organised and have a plan or routine. Aidan Jolly, a busy community musician and prolific singer-songwriter, suggests that if members of a band can be introduced to the concept of group dynamics—how any group forms, develops, peaks, levels off, and begins again in a cycle—then it can help them to survive the crisis moments, those times when things just ain't going right.

Here is a rehearsal exercise to do on your own as a 'thought experiment'. You have two hours to rehearse two new songs and run over an old one that didn't go so well on the last gig. The drummer is going to be late because her car has broken down, and the singer's mum is in hospital seriously ill. How do you divide the time? Whose role is it to plan the session? What would be the best (and worst) outcome?

Getting that crucial experience of live gigs, developing stagecraft and slick presentation, creating a 'look' and an identity: all this can b e assisted by a music facilitator. And it's great to watch as confidence grows and the band develops. Attention to 'extra-musical' questions can help here. How and when the band talk to the audience, what they say, whether they perform standing still (or even sitting), or 'go crazy' on stage—these are things that can make a difference in how a band is received by an audience, which in turn directly influences the morale (and hence the performance) of the musicians. They are also some of the aspects of performance that can be thought about during rehearsals.

Here are some rehearsal pointers for the band. Try setting up for rehearsal as if it is a gig, with the band all facing one way. Always arrange amps and equipment carefully, and check for tangled or trailing wires—do you know about 1970s bands Stone the Crows and Free? Each saw a member electrocuted. Gaffer tape loose ends. Monitor noise levels and keep them safe. (Find out about earplugs.) Have regular breaks when no-one plays, or when people can go into a quiet room. Have a friend video you in rehearsal or at a gig, and try to face yourselves honestly. What do you think you look like, as well as what do you sound like? Ask a good friend—someone whose critical judgement you trust—to give their opinions. Don't be precious—be silly, be daring, be adventurous, be creative. Watch the video at least twice, because each time you will see yourselves in different ways.

Pop Idle?

It takes time to play a 'real' instrument. Too many projects expect miracles in too short a space of time. Learning an instrument is a lifetime journey, but (as the proverbial wise person might say) this journey starts underneath your feet: with the first step. One of the most important aspects of community music generally is to provide the opportunity to start this journey. Bandwork probably begins (though as I have said above not necessarily) a few kilometres on, and can be an early peak in that journey. Band projects—if well organised—can provide lots of firsts: first set of songs, first performance, first dealings with managers, agents and venues, first recording, first radio broadcast and television appearance, and so on. They can also serve to set out the real challenges involved in continuing this journey. The most effective band projects I have been involved with have always included longer term vision. They have provided advice and direction from seasoned musicians, promoters and record labels, from Musicians' Union officers, and plenty of signposts to further destinations such as colleges and universities that offer music courses. They have included examples of other bands' stories, with contractual wrangles and arguments over who wrote what percentage of what. They categorically have not promised easy fame and fortune. After participating in such a project, young people have a better idea of whether or not (and how) they want to continue. Some people find their musical path, and a personal commitment to it. Others realise they have to prioritise other things (jobs, other interests, schooling) and relegate music-making to a part-time hobby. Others again enjoy themselves but decide they are 'not musicians'. All of these outcomes are positive.

Bands do require access to their own kit. Bandwork with people who cannot practice is very difficult if not impossible. Access to instruments and, thereafter, good tuition, are crucial. Because of this, two possibilities open up. On the one hand, projects work with people who can already play, and focus on how to develop a group sound and approach. Here there is the potential advantage that the musicians can practice individually and rehearse away from the project time. In this case it is possible to set tasks and challenges to be worked on between sessions. It should go without saying that musical progress will be easier, and end results will reflect this. On the other hand, instruments can be provided and participants encouraged to have a go and see what they can do. Sometimes the very act of providing access to, say, a loud and fairly unwieldy instru-

ment such as a full drum kit, next to a bass guitar plugged into an amp, is in itself demystifying, liberating and powerful. If project participants do not own their own instruments (sometimes the case with youth music projects intent on providing 'first time experiences') the process and outcome will be different. Community musicians will have to rely on the instruments available, and whatever they choose to bring themselves.

Sometimes the quality of these instruments will be suspect, and in any case they should be checked over before giving them out. Health and safety concerns include broken sharp bits, dodgy electrical connections and germs. (I always carry a box of antiseptic wipes for instruments with mouth pieces.) Where instruments are provided for first-timers, a good deal of project time will be taken up playing with them, exploring what they do and the sounds they make. At this stage, a healthy balance between the tutor demonstrating the conventional playing techniques and encouraging participants' freestyle exploration is good. It takes time and patience to learn the proper technique for playing any instrument, but, with the right attitude, no time at all to make sounds which can be worked together into a composition.

In a project I facilitated in Derbyshire I gave an electric guitar to a participant, showed her how to get a sustaining distorted sound, and encouraged her to experiment with the tremolo arm ('whammy bar'). The results were epic, and required little conventional technique. This very fluid sound was set against simple interlocking drum patterns and a melody played on a keyboard that was marked with coloured numbered stickers. At one point in the piece, the keyboard's drum machine was used, with the participant controlling the tempo and volume. The overall result was a five minute piece of music that had an intense filmic quality, i.e. enough changes of atmosphere that it hinted at a story. None of the participants had played those particular instruments before, but during performance to a large group of their peers played with confidence and conviction.

When I have a project with several participants who can play (and who own) their instruments, I try to mix them with those who don't. When this works, the instrumentalists actually pass on their skills to their peers in a better way than I could, and each sub-group of participants benefits by having someone who can provide an element of stability and confidence. The danger is that the others feel like second fiddle, relegated to the simple tasks of, for example, tambourine shaking or cowbell bashing. Two things here: firstly, if the music requires tambourine or cowbell, I make it clear that it is just as crucial as lead guitar or keyboards, and that these apparently simply percussive or decorative instruments require just as much skill and concentration as any others. (Think of Motown tambourine, or the bell patterns of samba, or the salsa band leaders who front the band with a pair of maracas.) Secondly, I try to make sure that everyone p l a y s more than one part in the course of the workshop. For example, I will introduce an 'a capella' piece, or a drumming piece, something where everyone is on a more level playing field. I also repeatedly stress the co-operative element of music-making, the teamwork aspect. Not everyone can be the soloist or singer standing in the spotlight; just as important are the other players who work together to help the singer or soloist's sound make the overall music better. (It is worth remembering that even rivalry and tension rely on some sort of group profile to generate the creative spark.)

A project in Rochdale combined fairly experienced players with complete beginners. One piece came from a freestyle 'have a go' session, when two girls sat together at a drumkit and played it in two halves—one played hi-hat, snare and crash cymbal, the other played bass drum, tom toms and ride cymbal. They devised a distinctive rhythm (in three-four time) which led to another piece of music. One boy was quite skilled on electric guitar, another on bass, and together with first-timers on keyboards, drum machine and percussion a song emerged, which was then sung by three girls who had never used microphones before. The initial freestyle session—completely free improvisation—sounded extremely chaotic and loud, but it generated at least two seed ideas. Several of the participants had Attention Deficit Disorder, one had been expelled more than once from primary school, and we had been warned about the 'lively and challenging' nature of the group (or words to that effect). There was a final performance which was confidently played and musically successful, and impressed the parents who came to see almost as much as the youth workers who had warned us.

5

Much of the bandwork you are likely to do will be youth related. The National Foundation of Youth Music has, since its launch in 1 9 9 9 , done valuable work promoting music-making for young people, and this advocacy has helped to demystify the work. However, it is wise not to assume that project managers from youth services, community organizations or councils know what you can do, and you should tell them yourself whenever possible. But pop and rock music has been around for half a century — and that means that the surviving early rock 'n' rollers are veteran pensioners now, while the bands of the sixties and seventies might themselves be entering their sixties and seventies. Can you still be in a band once you pass the age of 25 (or 35, or 45)? Of course you can. It may become more d i f-ficult to make a living, other things such as children or (non-musical) career can encroach, but if you love music-making, remember that to stop might be more damaging than to find ways to continue! And like older blues musicians, say, ' what you lose in speed you make up for with guile and experience. '

In my experience, the impact of new technologies on bandwork cuts two ways. Incorporating new technologies into music-making is a challenge. Getting people out of their lonely bedrooms and studios and into the social situation of a band is a challenge. Technology can swallow interaction, as everyone gazes into the screen and fights for control of the mouse. But it can enable people with no instrumental skills to be full creative members of the band by using live software or decks. How it is used needs to be thought about. It has become easier to record fairly good quality demos or even CDs for sale, w h i c h can help with a band's cashflow. But traditional recording engineer skills are still essential here. Longer-term bandwork projects could bring in recording engineers to work with the participants, perhaps even as co-producers, discussing and advising approaches to capturing the band sound.

Conclusion: my personal bandwagon

I have played instruments since I was six years old—that's over thirty years. Beginning with recorder, then trombone, and then—inspirationally—guitar at the age of 12. The guitar was my greatest love, and I gave up the trombone (and the brass band I played in) to study classical guitar and electric guitar. The former entailed reading music and learning the canon of classical guitar pieces, taking grade exams and playing in a classical guitar ensemble, all of which I enjoyed. However, the electric guitar quickly became my main interest, and opened up the possibility of playing in rock and pop bands. My teenage musical influences were mostly rock and punk bands, and I aspired to play in one myself. This seemed radical in many respects. Instead of simply learning correct fingering and the stylistic niceties of playing baroque and classical Spanish music, there was the freedom to interpret chord symbols and experiment with melodic solos in a more directly expressive and creative way. And of course, it increased the number of other musicians I could play with, because it was not necessary that they were able to read music, just to have a good grasp of their instrument. It also opened up the possibility of writing my own songs. So began a personal musical journey that continues still. I have played in many bands, and more recently, as part of my teaching duties in schools and colleges, worked with bands to help them develop. As I wrote earlier, I found producing this 'bandwagon' an enjoyable and reflective process, and would recommend it as an exercise for any musician who has been in more than a couple of bands. You will learn something about yourself, and about music. It may be particularly useful for those musicians who are (as actors say) 'resting' between gigs and bands—think of it as a morale booster rather than a litany of failure though…

1981 (age 16yrs), Liverpool. Nothing Yet
A band that formed with friends from school and through a wider social network. We wrote our own songs, but also discussed what covers we might do. I don't remember which ones—if any—we did. Good experience, good fun, but never got out of the living room. Named by my nan who asked what we were called. I replied, 'Nothing yet'. She said she thought it was a good name. Lesson one: got to start somewhere.

5

1982, Annapolis Royal, Nova Scotia, Canada

Due to my parents changing their careers my family emigrated to Canada. Music was an important factor in making new friends. I played in the High School band, but more importantly formed a rock band with some of my new friends. I can't remember what we called ourselves but we rehearsed in a seafood restaurant owned by the bass player's parents (and got a good clam chowder if we were lucky). We only performed a few times, but I do recall a charity fundraiser gig being broadcast by a local radio show.

1983, back in Liverpool

No bands but lots of writing songs and swapping them with others at parties and such like. Met—through my brother, who was good friends with him—John Power, who went on to be the bass player in The La's and then to form Cast. Was inspired by Lee Mavers, who played an intense solo version of 'There She Goes' in our living room, before our few eyes, and went on to fame with The La's.

1985, Sussex University, Brighton

Although I was there to study History, being a musician opened more (and more interesting) doors. Have guitar will jam. Lots of solo, duo and band gigs—mostly at parties, political demos and benefit gigs. O n c e played for several hours to a bunch of environmental protestors who had chained themselves to heavy machinery. I hope it helped keep their spirits up!

1990, Morocco

'Oh, you are a musician? You must come and meet my friend Abdul'. So off we go, and so began one of the most memorable nights of my life. Let's just say a few Cat Stevens songs led to an all-night Gnawa trance session with three musicians assisting the ecstasy of many dancers. Never has music seemed so directly powerful.

1990, Brighton. Waterwheel

A folk-rock band that boasted two PhD science students, a computer programmer, and a sweet-voiced under-grad. Talk about over-qualified. Developed a live set that regularly attracted full houses in the small venues we played around Brighton, and made two studio albums released independently on cassette. I wrote the title track of the second album 'Return'.

1991, Brighton. Scat Attack
Not strictly speaking a band but a pub duo performing jazz classics from the 40's and a few of our own. Think Louis Jordan meets The Proclaimers—though we never set out to do that!

1992-93, Brighton. Urban Desert Orchestra
A collective of musicians and dancers performing extemporisations on traditional Egyptian dance tunes. At one point we performed with an Egyptian, a Madagascan, an Israeli, an Italian-Spaniard brought up in England and half-a-dozen others from around Britain. We performed at Glastonbury Festival (what a buzz!) as well as the Brighton Festival. I learned about the travel of music and culture from northern India via the Arab world to Spain—from Hindustani to Flamenco—and soaked up melodies and rhythms that have been played in Egypt for centuries.

1991-4, Brighton. One Big Party
A reggae band playing originals written by a very talented singer. I was in at the beginning of this one, which became locally a great success, winning a battle of the bands competition, getting interest from the Acid Jazz label and after many south coast gigs doing a two-week tour of France and Czechoslovakia. We went through about three different line-ups, and worked with several promoters and managers. In the end the deal never came off, and despite a strong local following sustaining the band proved too difficult. Then I left Brighton.

1995-6, Leeds. Bassa Bassa
A 'world music jazz big band', being a rather flexible line-up playing jazz, ska, Latin and tangos. Lots of fun, a fair few gigs and hugely useful for meeting other musicians and learning new stuff. Not one for beginners, as the material was quite demanding. Fortunately my previous experiences stood me in good stead.

1997, Basildon. Unnamed band
Ultimately not my scene, but better than nothing, and provided some relief from the stress of being a music teacher in a large comprehensive school.

2001, Manchester. Cuchillo
Featuring a top session singer let loose on the lead, a creative bassist and a very funky sax player, on compositions inspired by Steely Dan and 70's soulful funk. All grown up and too busy to do the regular band thing, and because we weren't quickly spotted and signed up for a lucrative deal, we managed 18 months and half a dozen gigs. Still, the recordings we made still sound good, including the live ones. And I'm not sure what kind of 'deal' would have made sense for us anyway, given that we were all so busy with other things.

2003, Manchester. The Rubber Bucket Band
Put together for the sole purpose of entertaining the guests at a friend's wedding party, we played a medley of cheesy covers relevant to the occasion. Three rehearsals and the gig was the lifespan of this band.

When I think about these bands, and my part in them, I realise how much I got out of them, how many switched-on people I met through them and how much I learned about myself and others, above and beyond any musical learning. In some cases, especially as a y o u n g e r man, a band made a sort of surrogate family—which certainly helped me overcome the untimely death of my mother. Through the various styles and genres covered by these bands I went on a musical voyage, and whenever I did physically travel abroad, being a musician was a passport into the heart of other places and cultures. And whereas playing and singing on my own—practising, writing songs or simply playing for enjoyment—has always been a necessary and fulfilling thing to do, playing with others has many times brought about a transcendental magic that I struggle to put into words. At its best that's what being in a band is all about. When I think about bandwork, and my involvement with it, I see this as a very closely related music-making activity. Claire Mooney, a busy singer-songwriter and community musician, was told she could be a community musician or an artist in her own right, but not both. She did not accept the advice and has successfully combined both roles for many years. In Mooney's view, if you don't regularly perform and record yourself, you can lose touch with the process. It is important to practice what you preach, especially if the young people you work with can see and hear you. Further, it may refresh and inspire you. I agree with this absolutely, and personally continue to take all the opportunities that come my way for performance and collaboration. Because I love making music with people.

Acknowledgements

Thanks to the many musicians I've worked with over the years at Band on the Wall, High Peak Community Arts, Urban Voice, Community Arts NW, Access to Music, Drake Music Project, Contact Theatre, The Lowry, Backdoor Music Project, the Hallé, and more. We learn from each other as we travel. Also, a 'big up' for the non-musicians who have made so much happen: the youth workers, project leaders, mini-bus drivers, caretakers,... Finally, my particular thanks to Aidan Jolly and Claire Mooney for agreeing to be interviewed for this chapter.

MOVING IMAGES

You only see a moving image because the eye plays the film
Depending on your mechanics it's all fast forward or slow motion
Imagine you could capture the image in your digital self
Try it. Catch a look. Capture the brush of colour
Catch a ribbon of smoke as it melts…

The gentle ripples that push through the air as each person speaks
Watch those ripples as they corrugate the world and gather in the sky
It will rain poems. It will rain songs. Seagulls become lyric sheets
And clouds become notes giving strength to the weak
Rain clouds are the great scripts of the sky
And rainbows are the poems and songs
Try it. Catch a falling start and write yourself the world
Write a ribbon of hope and ride on.

chapter 6
Voicing heart, mind and body
by Katherine Zeserson

Be(com)ing a voice worker

Singing is completely natural—this is obvious but of crucial importance. Our bodies are the instruments. I believe that singing is an evolutionary necessity—it derives from the infant's cry, and it is our own personal poetry of survival. No one needs to learn to sing; we can only improve our singing, learning to play the instrument better, to sing new things, to extend our voices. If we do not sing, or think we can not, then we have been obstructed, repressed or scared out of it.

Many of us need to unlearn barriers to singing. Watch babies vocalise, observe the effectiveness of their vocal communication. We all had that once. Most of our business as voice and song workers is about helping people to remove the barriers that have grown up between themselves and the optimum, free use of their voices.

6

There are habits that need to be undone:

- **habits of breathing** - tight, shallow
- **habits of mind** - 'who do I think I am to do this'
- **habits of posture** - slumped, curved
- **habits of communication** - half closed mouth, slight frown.

Much of our work is about reminding the body of what it already knows—the infant breath, the running posture, the belly laugh, the sharp ear, the flexible lips, the need to be heard. There is a paradox here. The instrument is intimate and personal, the sound it produces is not only public, but is a key tool of our survival. When dealing with the voices of others therefore, we must work with our greatest compassion, respect and sensitivity.

We speak, we sing, we vocalise, we are silent. We do all of these to communicate, connect and manifest ourselves. We have a family of voices to choose from, and that family grows with us. The voice worker helps people experience the connection between the speaking, singing and silent voices so that people realise they are not learning something new, simply re-connecting to or extending what they already know. The voice worker seeks to enable a confident exploration of possibilities, to encourage and inspire people to reach for their full self through and from their voices, and to impart information and technical knowledge to support that aspiration-singing for the first time in a community choir, working on upper register intonation in order to sing an operatic line more beautifully, writing a rap, joining a barbershop quartet, raising your voice to be heard in discussion, having the confidence to sing to or with your children, learning to breathe freely and sing without a sore throat......you fill in the gaps. The other community musicians I spoke to about this chapter have an approach to work with voices that is grounded in the physical base, exploring and liberating the voice in the body-strengthening the instrument and learning the art of playing it to its best.

Being a voice worker is a bit like working for a roadside rescue firm-people are so pleased to see you. You engage in psychical midwifery, alchemy, psychology, body work, musical direction, teaching, information sharing, artistry, poetry, dance, consciousness-raising, leadership, philosophical enquiry, challenging, directing, nurturing, healing, partying.... An inspiring and liberating voice leader needs a well-grounded understanding of how voices work, an open-minded interest in what they can be used for, passionate musicality, skill and confidence in playing their own voice, and a delight in enabling others to make progress.

I work with people's awareness of their voices—how does it feel, how does it sound—so that they can become adept at tuning into and then directing that complex, precise mechanism, and so that they feel playful, inspired and confident about their unique instrument. I aim to create an exploratory, open-minded research environment wherever I work with voices—choir practices, workshops, training sessions—so that we are happy to look inside analytically and imaginatively, to discover 'what happens if I ...', and then share those sounds and insights. I propose that we: animate the body, open the mind, explore the voice, raise aspiration, inspire courage, make great music, share and celebrate. Not always in that order, not always explicit, not always all of that all at once; but those are the fixed points in the background of my moving picture. For I have a rather utopian view, you see: singing is an act of generosity.

The more you understand how voices work, the easier it is for you to enable others. It is not about learning to control our voices, rather learning to control the mechanism that produces them, in order to play the instrument well in order to free the voice. Immerse yourself—find out how voices are used and developed in singing traditions that are not your own, read about physiology, investigate different systems of teaching—so that you become well informed about your instrument, and use all of this information to develop your own approach and style of leadership. Develop your detective skills, so you can respond to people's questions or difficulties by helping them track down the roots of the problem. Sing many different things in many different ways. Listen to singing styles you do not like and try to understand how they work. Experiment on yourself—try out some operatic exercises for range, teach yourself a Lebanese song (if you are not Lebanese), investigate tai chi breathing exercises.

6

See what happens if I...

Find some friends to do these things with—form or join a network. Sharing experiences, repertoire, techniques and approaches is the very best way to develop your practice. It is also the case that our craft grows in complexity, artistry and usefulness through collaborative investigation and experimentation. Build time into your work schedule for this; give it the same importance as the sessions you lead for others. Where you can, include the cost of your professional development time in your fees.

The voice and the instrument (the body)

• We can not see the voice, so we have to imagine it.

• Use imagery, encourage people to find their own. What colour is this sound—pink, green, mottled? Where is this sound coming from—your back, your feet, your nose? What is its texture—velvet, sand, mud? Encourage people to imagine texture, colour, shape and then sing it.

• Encourage people to explore text and feeling—is this sound angry, loving, lost, contented, humorous? What does it feel like? Can I reproduce that? What is my body doing when it sounds like that? Use drama exercises and poetry in improvisation to find out how sound conveys meaning.

• We can amass knowledge from describing our experiences—'it felt warm here when I did that and it sounded rich', 'it felt tight here when I did that and it sounded squeaky', and so on.

• The more we explore and play, the more knowledge we amass about the instrument, the greater the range of voices we can choose to use because we have mapped our voices on the landscape of our bodies.

• It becomes unconscious: I imagine singing soft, yellow, gentle tenderness and my muscles make the necessary adjustments. I am singing a text that expresses anger: my muscles make the necessary adjustments. We do it when speaking so we can do it when singing. We just need to establish the connections.

• The more you use your voice, the stronger it becomes.

• As for the body, singing is internal dancing. It is athletic. We just can't see all the parts of the body that are working.

• Muscles control and support breath. Breath activates vocal chords. Bones and skeletal cavities resonate sound. Strong, exercised muscles are easier to direct; the more precisely you can direct your muscles the easier it is to manage the flow of air across the cords.

• Physical fitness and general well-being will always make the instrument easier to play.

Working with a group of voices and bodies

Relaxed alertness is the optimum physiological and psychological condition for singing—muscles are ready to work, but not so tight they are muffling the resonator (skeleton). To get to that condition, we can prepare. This is the 'warm up'. The purpose of the warm-up is to get ready for doing what ever it is we are planning to do. It will always be helpful to prepare the instrument (body) for sustained singing and vocal work through some combination of warming, stretching, loosening and flexing. It will always be helpful to prepare the vocal mechanism through some combination of unfocused and focused sounds, gently working the cords, releasing the breath, activating the jaw, tongue and so on, focusing the ear through imitation of phrases, and so on.

Encourage exploration. Work with gibberish, work from speaking and then exaggerate the pitch differences, slow it down, speed it up. Work with mimicry, work from movement—sing the sound of a gesture. Where physically able, try working on the floor, with feet flat and knees drawn up. Release long notes to the ceiling and enjoy the freedom. Or sing upside down—dropping the body down by folding at the pelvis and bending the knees whilst sliding up the voice. Feel the release. Overall, it can be very productive to use movement—take each other's voices for a walk by 'leading' a partner round the room indicating shape and character and up/down of sound by hand movements. Try dancing and singing at the same time, or running and singing. But, if it hurts, stop, check and change: this is not a 'no pain, no gain' business.

There are hundreds of activities, exercises and pieces of musical material that will liberate and strengthen voices and help people learn to control the mechanism. They come from singing teaching, from voice work, from dance, from traditional and composed repertoire bases, from yoga, from sport, from theatre. Devise your own exercises and materials as well as using those you have enjoyed and found helpful. Decide what you are aiming to achieve then figure out an activity that addresses it. Test it out. Gather feedback from the group. Adjust. Test again. Gather more feedback. Liberating and strengthening the voice, and achieving an increased ability to control the mechanism, will follow from repetition—vocal exercises or vocal exploration just needs to be done regularly; we do not need to 'get better' at it. We are helping the body extend and develop new habits of behaviour.

In the workshop/choir practice/music session you are running, good beginnings make all the difference. Why are we here in this room? People's reasons for coming to sing are complex and varied; they often may not even have articulated why they have come, either, so you have to work with all possibilities, whether acknowledged or not. People come to voice or singing activities to:

> take a risk
> discover or develop their voices
> enjoy singing a particular kind of music
> enjoy singing anything
> learn new songs
> feel part of something
> meet people

You will encounter other motivations too though.
They are here because:

> they have to be (school, prison, hospital)
> their mates are
> they are bored
> the session is happening in their youth club
> they are lonely

So, you have to work with all possible motives, whether they have been acknowledged by the individual or not, whether they have been shared with you or not.

You need to establish yourself as a trustworthy person. People need to feel that you know what you're doing, and that you are committed to their flourishment, so they will be happy to follow your lead. Sometimes this is difficult—there may be someone in a group who makes you feel uncomfortable—so you need to focus on hearing that voice and making wise choices about activities that will enable its growth. It is not about you. Pay attention constantly: keep looking around the room, check body posture, facial expression. Notice people's fears and their pride, so you can include both their skills and their doubts. You also need to establish a clear framework. Whatever the task at hand—rehearsing the parts for Bach's B Minor Mass, enabling a group of people at their first Find Your Voice session to make sound and enjoy it, developing improvisation skills in a community choir—it is easier for people to find the best in themselves if they are secure in the situation and know what the parameters are, what the culture is.

With new groups, or one-off sessions, or at the beginning of a new block of work with a group I know well, I like to do a quick check to understand individual goals. Sometimes it works well simply to ask people to say what they are expecting, and to write all of those things down, giving the group an agenda. These may vary from 'Don't know, just thought I'd have a go' to 'improve my voice', 'learn some Irish songs', 'find out my range', 'become more confident'. The agenda can then be referred back to throughout the process to help people realise the progress they are making, and to help you remember to focus activities so that those goals will be met. You need to be honest here—if you end up with things on the list that in your professional judgement probably can not be achieved in the day or across the ten sessions, or that you do not want to do, then negotiate at this stage.

You can take these individual goals and summarise them for the group so there is common cause: 'We can go through some basic technique that will help with all of the things people have mentioned, and focus on different aspects of voice each week to make sure each individual question is answered', or 'People can move around within the songs so that everyone gets a chance to see what it is like to use a different part of their range', and so on. Groups that know you and each other well get used to this kind of process and learn to use it effectively, sharing goals explicitly. For instance, 'We all want to improve our ears—let's learn some more challenging contemporary music'; 'We all have weakness in the upper end of the voice—let's do some technical work on that'; 'We want to come first in Eisteddfod this year—let's pick repertoire we think gives us the best chance of that.' Such group cohesion can be a very rewarding creative learning experience for the group and the community musician alike.

Sometimes it does not feel right to spend time at the beginning of the session in discussion. This may be because the group is too big and it would take too long, or because you want to create a high-energy feeling in the room from the start, or perhaps you sense that there are people in the group who will not feel able to answer such direct questions about their own learning, or perhaps the group is not there voluntarily and so people will not yet have discovered that there are things they can learn and enjoy here. Then you can share a structure, by which I mean saying something like:

So this is an improvisation workshop. My idea is that we spend some time finding out how our voices work and how we control and influence the sounds we make, and then some time experimenting, having a play with what we find, and then we can work with some written structures— blues and jazz songs—as well as inventing some new music of our own. Nobody will have to sing on their own if they don't want to, but you will be very welcome to if you'd like. I'll be asking us to do some exercises and activities which you may find unfamiliar, or daft—I'm asking you to trust me on this—I'll tell you the purpose of each exercise, and it will never be to make you feel stupid! Okay?

Be clear, and be a leader—it's your job. On other occasions it feels right to say absolutely nothing—but you are still leading, offering guidance with clarity and purpose. You establish quiet in the room, you direct people to stand in a circle, or a half moon, you point to yourself and make a gesture or a vocalisation, then you point to the group to invite mimicry. Gradually the group grasps the game, and you lead the first phase of your day/workshop/session just using the voice and the body. At the end of that phase you can invite respones, q u e s t i o n s, reflections and then set out your stall.

Some further thoughts about voice leadership

• Try it all ways round—do it your way, investigate, learn, test things out. Do not be frightened to change your approach. Ask questions. Aim for 'and' rather than 'but', which allows you to include contributions, and therefore contributors, in the same frame of reference, even when you disagree with them.

• All vocal situations can encompass all goals: a very formal choir practice can be a place where people discover a whole new facet of their timbre and hence are freer to communicate feeling in their singing. A singing-for-the-terrified-workshop can be a place people sing a little Bach for the first time and discover that the group loves polyphony. And so on. You enable that to happen.

• Use positive language—for instance, not 'This is quite hard, so don't worry if you can't do it', rather 'We'll take this in sections and give it time, because it's a challenge for us'.

• Engage people in a range of different kinds of activities in one session: song learning, improvising and technical exercises; or very still, focused work and then some dancing; or work with grooves and then work with words.

• Make the most of our multiple intelligence. Use movement, visual and spatial metaphors, mathematical and structural imagery, analytical reasoning, emotional language.

• Commit to people taking responsibility for their own learning and share what you have in support of that. If you are asked a how-to question always try and answer it, even if the answer is 'I don't know, but I'll do some research for you' or 'I don't know, perhaps you could do some research for us about that.' Don't hide your ignorance, keep musical secrets, or withhold the 'key' to the technique till the end of the workshop; it's disempowering. If you find yourself doing that, then check with yourself what it is you feel insecure or unconfident about, recognise your own learning need and meet it—through your network, through your research, through self-reflection. You will feel insecure and unconfident some times and that's the mark of an awake and aware leader. Just take responsibility for dealing with it and try not to let it spill out on your group.

Whichever way you begin, focus, clarity and pace are your responsibility.

Keep it going—this does not mean being manic, rather purposeful, resourceful, inventive. The group is in a process of questioning, testing, discovery, exploration, and the group is a collection of i n d i v i d u- als, each working to his or her own rhythm. You have to gather up the individual threads and knit them together, balancing the needs of individual and group. You have to decide when to move on from rep- etitions of that phrase and on to the next, when to move on from breath-based exercises to tone-based exercises, when to pause and invite reflection, when to stop and change. You do this by constantly holding the aims and goals of the event as the bedrock of all your choices, making decision minute-by-minute on the basis of your experience and your best judgment as to which next intervention will best move the group forward in pursuance of their aims.

You have a good deal of power here, especially when individual aims have not been articulated, or owned up to, and you have taken responsibility for determining underlying collective aims in a 'best interest' way. For example, if working with a group of school-refusing teenagers, using singing is a means of enabling self-reflection, self- confidence, greater ownership of the body; it is an activity at which these young people can excel and become skilled as opposed to their experiences in school. Remember, you are working with peo- ple's voices, their undressed souls, and the consequences of misus- ing that power are great. But do not be afraid. Rather, stay clear about the purpose, and establish short term collective aims 'We could write a song together, or I could teach you one, or some of you could make up a dance to a song you all know, what do you think?' so that you have established a visible common goal or goals that everyone can feel responsible for and excited about.

I emphasise again the need to stay attentive to the group, and be driven by that. If it starts to feel wrong then you can pause and change it, saying, for instance, 'Actually maybe we won't keep trying to learn this line, people aren't getting a lot out of this. Let's leave it and move on to something else'. It is not about you, so you can be quite free to reveal your choices and decisions, wise and unwise, without shame. Be guided by the group, without leaving them unsupported or lacking in focus. Listen to the voices, to the singing, and keep proposing activities and ideas that enable people's skills to improve and their self-direction to grow, without requiring individual attention or public acknowledgement of error. You hear that there are one or two voices in the soprano section that are well sharp. So you lead intonation exercises focusing on the upper register for a few weeks at the beginning of each session. Then when rehearsing the piece again you remind the whole choir to use the feeling and learning they gained through the exercise. On another occasion, you are working in a school, and notice that a couple of teenage boys keep moving to the back of the group, shuffling around, and when they are singing are only able to offer a monotone. You add some lively vocalisations to the piece you are working on that only use vocal percussion, drones and spoken voice. You make sure that those boys are free to choose these roles in the piece without drawing attention to themselves, and you affirm how much that part contributes to the good sound of the whole.

You need to feel comfortable and authentic about your facilitation, direction or leadership, but whatever your style, people will have the most valuable, developmental and positive experience if you can establish a culture of shared enquiry, in which all vocalisation and responses to the process are not just acceptable, but essential, as data for our research. 'I'd like you to start with a low hum, right at the bottom of your range, and gradually raise the pitch and the volume to a free shout. Don't worry if your voice cracks or screeches—we're just finding out what happens. We'll all be making completely different kinds of sounds.' Then when the exercise has been repeated a few times, you can ask: 'What did anyone notice? Were there particular areas of pitch where particular things happened?' And someone might reply: 'It just closed up when I got high. It sounded horrible'. You might then say: 'No problem, we weren't looking for a particular kind of sound, just finding out what sound came. Did that closing up feeling happen to anyone else?' The reply to this will undoubtedly be 'Yes!' Then: 'So let's explore that. Let's all sing (demonstrate pitch, or melody or whatever you decide to use for the exercise) and see what happens if we (hang our heads, do it quietly, do it loudly etc.)'

In this kind of way you establish a culture in which we can all jointly gather information and then use it as we each individually see fit. We learn through an open dialogue. Everything is useful to everyone. In this example, what will happen is that people will discover the effect of changing their posture on the relative ease or discomfort with which they can produce sound, and its quality of open-ness, its intonation and its timbre. The 'best place' will be slightly different for everyone depending on things like musculature, skeletal habits, physical history. But the idea behind it—that posture affects vocal sound—is true for all of us, and there is no value judgement embedded either in the process of discovery, or the proposition we formulate: posture affects voice. Therefore, if I want to change the sound of my voice in any way it may be useful to investigate my posture, and so the question of its horribleness or not becomes irrelevant to the process of my learning how to play my instrument.

You are inviting people to find out what they can be and do, and they cannot be wrong in exploring that. Unfortunately, they will often think they are—our education system in general and our culture of singing in particular are loaded with value judgements, punishment-based control systems and a lack of respect for the commitment of individuals to their own and each other's development. (A related point here is that people will often expect you to judge them and you may need to be extra aware of this in the first few sessions with a new group.) Clearly, people make mistakes and people can improve. So, if you are teaching a song and you hear a persistent error in a particular part, you can say: 'I think the alto line you are singing isn't exactly what we learned/I have asked for.' You demonstrate the line that is wanted (because it is what Bach wrote, because it is what we made up together, because it is how that song is always sung), and then the one that is being sung, point out the difference, and choose an effective way of making the change so people are accurate. It is only 'wrong' in so far as it is not what the group has agreed. This applies equally to the B Minor Mass, the Irish song and the one we made up earlier in the workshop.

There is a serious physiological basis for taking this approach; it is not just about kindness. Because the body is the instrument, its condition directly affects the sound it makes. If I think I am wrong or bad, then I feel tense and sad and fearful of punishment.

My throat tightens, my breathing becomes shallow and I prepare for fight or flight. I lose control of the vocal mechanism, my mind panics and I cannot imagine the sound I am trying to make. It all goes downhill. If on the other hand I am simply choosing between line X which we have agreed to sing and line Y which I am singing, then I just need to investigate the difference and figure out what to do about it. It is interesting and creative, I learn something and I have no fear. I do not panic. I am not wrong.

People have ears and good sense and do not want to be patronised or lied to. If we are working on a particular song, we want to sound good. We all have a rough or perhaps even very precise idea about what that means. Your job as voice worker is to help us get there. When you have the trust of the group, it really is fine to say 'It's very out of tune in that part, and you're all speeding up dreadfully', or 'I'm not hearing the dynamics', as long as you then offer a suggestion or some guidance as to how to improve the situation. This may be: 'Just check your head and neck posture, loosen your jaws, remember the feeling of airiness around the notes, and maybe look down a little?' Or it may be: 'Pay attention—I'm conducting here! Watch me closely and I'll give really clear signals for the dynamic change'. We are jointly engaged in the collaborative task of making this sound as good as we can: it is a problem-solving exercise, not a fault-finding one.

The choral conductor and singing teacher who shout at people, who criticise individuals in front of the group, or who make explicit value judgements about voices are not just unpleasant; they are creating the conditions in which it is hard for learning to happen and for improvements to be made. Unconfident people will leave, confident people who can cope with the abuse will probably develop poor technique and vocal strain—how many members of choirs and singing groups run in this way 'lose their voices' as they get older? Don't you be responsible for adding to that refrain drain.

Some thoughts and guidance about repertoire

• Explore, improvise, devise, create. Use exploration exercises to lead into improvisation. Use words to create melodies. Use rhythms and grooves, layer things up. Use drones to explore harmony. Encourage musical choices with your groups—shall we do this or that?—and through that create new repertoire.

• People like to learn and sing songs, so you need to have some you can teach; if you are teaching a song, you need to know it—even if you only taught it to yourself the night before.

• Pay attention to the group's interest and responses, and as well as bringing material you are sure people will like, do not be afraid to propose and pursue repertoire people may be uncertain about at first. Enlist people in working it through before rejecting it.

• Feel confident about sharing your own perspective on what you are or are not happy to sing and encourage the people you work with to share theirs. Explore these ideas.

• Broaden horizons, both your own and those of the people you are working with. Keep trying material that is outside your usual frame of reference.

• Respect material without being scared of it. If teaching a song from a culture or genre unfamiliar to you make sure you know its meaning, its original sound quality and feel, and if you make changes to those, know why.

• Songs are great vehicles for technical development, so think about range, the demands that harmonies will make on people's intonation, how rhythm may lead you into movement work. Illustrate points you have made during warm-up or technique sessions through the teaching of songs. Choose repertoire that works to the strengths and weaknesses of your group, so they both feel successful and challenged at the same time.

• Don't bang on at things—let the song cook. Teach a section; work on it until people start to look weary, then put it in the oven and do something completely different; easier, or more familiar, or playful. Get it out at the end of the session, or next week. It will either have settled and improved, or at least people will have fresh energy for the challenge.

• Songs inspire and communicate feelings. Choose songs that make you laugh, or dance, or cry; songs that connect, that explore issues people have in common, that support and celebrate; songs that challenge, that respond to the world we live in or the things that are happening around us, or that come from completely different cultures and yet speak to our hearts.

• Teach repertoire imaginatively: try out different ways of singing. Impose contradictory styles—try a gospel song in a punk voice, a madrigal as a country and western tune in order to get deeper inside the meaning and the sonic potential. If the group has the physical capacity, sing lying on the floor with eyes closed; sing standing back to back. Gaze at the mouth and eyes of someone who is singing a different part. Walk around the room and hear how the harmonies sounds different. Run and sing and see what happens to your communication. Speak the text to your neighbour. Encourage aliveness—songs are three-dimensional sonic landscapes for us to explore.

• Attend to the text. Suggest and discuss the idea that to sing a song 'well' we need to mean it. At the same time, we can sing a song 'well' that we do not believe or agree with. For instance, we can act, we can adopt the mantle of the other, we can fit in with a group of people—and it can be a very illuminating, or fun, or sociable experience. We can also sing things we passionately care to communicate. It is important just that we know which we are doing and have consciously elected.

• Create your own repertoire. Find songs you love and rearrange them with your group or for your group. Take liberties. Change the time signature, the voicing, the rhythm. *Mess about.*

6

Conclusion
as a voice worker, enjoy yourself

Be brave, be clear, be rigorous. Have high musical standards, expect the best from the people who attend your workshops, help them to achieve it by manifesting a calm, cheerful presence; giving clear instructions; being patient; showing no blame or disappointment; thinking laterally and creatively; coming at things from different angles; changing the pace and rhythm of sessions in response to what happens; being fleet of foot, inventive in seeking new approaches and solutions to vocal and musical problems; being sure. Your surety gives strength, and strength leads to courage and confidence. Your faith in the potential of the group to develop and improve allows that to happen. If you do not believe in each group's potential, then the group will not achieve it. If you do, then it surely will.

Acknowledgements

Thanks to my parents for our singing home. Thanks to Sr. Mary Finan, late of Co. Sligo, Ireland, for starting me out on the path of this work through her loving vision of music in the spirit. Thanks to Richard Chew, Sian Croose and Carol Grimes for so generously informing both this chapter and my musical life with their insights, inspirational practice and comradeship.

RICH

It's scary to think that each day I can find
Gold in what I was told was a cold stone
mind. Inspiration doesn't go away. It's a home
It's waiting to be discovered—it's all here
Just half an hour a day… I crack that stone
And its vein of gold comes clear
It's wonderful to think each day I can find
Gold in what I was told was a cold mine.
I'm rich!

chapter 7

songmaking

by Pete Moser

Victor Jara of Chile
Lived like a shooting star
He fought for the people of Chile
With his songs and his guitar
And his hands were gentle
And his hands were strong.
Adrian Mitchell

Songs are everywhere. They exist in all cultures. We sing them, listen to them, use them to mark moments in our lives or the passing of time—from 'Happy birthday' to 'Auld lang syne'. Songs can send us to sleep, help us to calm down, songs can excite us and get us dancing. We remember songs and they bring back emotions and memories, we share songs with friends, songs have the power to focus a whole generation. So who makes songs and what are they made of… and why is it that they can be so powerful? I have had songs around me all my life and my relationship to them has changed in a number of phases from listener to performer to composer and teacher. In this chapter I aim to share my love of making songs and to give an insight into why they work and how anyone can make a song at some level.

At their most simple, songs consist of lyrics (words), melody and accompaniment (harmony/ instrumentation). But it is the character and mix of these that make the choice of each songmaker unique, and each song potentially special. Through this chapter I hope to show ways of creating melodies, discovering lyrics and making accompaniments whether by yourself or with others in groups. I will also refer to some of the many songmakers that I have worked with to create a set of tools that will help you make your own songs.

I grew up in the late sixties and early seventies listening to an enormous variety of popular songs from Dylan to the Beatles, from Buffalo Springfield and Stevie Wonder to Pink Floyd, the Rolling Stones and Soft Machine. At the same time in my home there was a great deal of classical music including a whole range of operatic music from Mozart to Benjamin Britten, Verdi, Wagner and Purcell. All of the songs I heard were made by composers and songwriters and composed in particular styles or genres and this raises my first question about songmaking: what tradition, what style, what world is the piece going to live within? As you develop personally you create your own style but when you start you inevitably acknowledge and make reference to a style, an idiom, a world of music.

From listening to songs I then moved into performing them in a variety of busking venues across London and Northern European cities. I could never remember the words (usually written on scraps of a paper on the top of the guitar) but the tunes, harmonies and chords were much easier. I started to write my own songs but there was no-one around to give advice and the results were wishy-washy lyrics, obvious structures and derivative chord sequences. In my late teens I travelled more extensively on the overland trail to Khatmandu and at some point on that trip decided that music was going to be central to my life. I needed to develop my skills and learning the trade involved understanding and analysis, discovering how other people made music, and developing my own language. This process of analysing and understanding other people's music started then for me, and has continued to this day. It has also become a vital teaching and com-positional tool.

I began to learn about composition at university studying a music degree but it was when I moved to Ulverston in Cumbria to work for the innovative theatre company, Welfare State International, that my songwriting really started. Within theatre there was an instant context and performance opportunity—there was a simplicity and power of song to capture people's hearts and minds and at WSI I met and began to work with three brilliant poets—Boris Howarth, Adrian Mitchell and John Fox. Each of them created lyrics in different styles, with different rhythmic nuances, different uses of language and metaphor, and I started writing hundreds of songs - for films, shows, celebrations and television. Often they would be themed together in small song cycles that allowed for harmonic and melodic connections and development.

With my arrival in Morecambe in the early 1990s I discovered the great joy of making songs with people, individually and in groups, and also the joy of teaching people how to run songwriting workshops themselves. A continuous run of projects has produced hundreds of songs, while a series of training weekends with expert songwriters such as Hugh Nankivell, Lemn Sissay, Mary Keith and Carol Grimes has helped me to formulate more strategies for songwriting. Unlike many of my friends I am always looking for a reason for a song to exist. Songs also arise just because you want them to - a story or an emotion that you feel like transforming into music, for instance - but for me I need a commission (whether for a set of songs for a theatre show or a birthday song for a relative). And particularly with group songmaking I always look for a theme and a context.

In fact I am always looking for opportunities to make songs on commission and at times have actually made this into the focus for a project. A song written for a specific person or place is very exciting. It can include personal information that is only relevant and interesting to that person and their friends/relatives but it can also touch on universal themes and ideas. The commissioned song can make a new connection into someone's life, open reflective doors for them and celebrate a moment in time in a unique fashion. Fusing emotional reaction and fine detail in a song is a powerful tool. Finding the right time and place to perform it can be tricky but can also focus an event such as a birthday in a lovely way. Of course, commissions come from all sorts of places and may not involve any financial transaction. There is no denying though that commissions do put some creative pressure on the songmaker too, to produce to a deadline!

7

Analyse this

As I have already argued, understanding songs really is a fundamental first step to making your own. The following list of questions can be used as a way of taking songs apart for yourself or in sessions with a group. The areas cover the musical content and the context. I am sure there are others you can come up with. By answering these sorts of questions you can become both a more attentive listener to songs and you can transfer that attention and knowledge to a group's or your own songmaking activity.

Structure
- Is there an intro/outro... verse/ chorus/ refrain?
- What repeats are there?
- What do you instantly recognise and remember?
- Is there a point when a number of aspects change?
- How long exactly is it?

Historical context and genre
- Identify the genre: country, R & B, rock n roll, hip hop, etc.
- Where are the roots of the style (country of origin, etc.)?
- What makes this genre specific (vocal style, instruments, lyrics)?
- What other artists make similar songs?
- What is the key audience?

Rhythm
- What is the beat? Can you sing it as a rhythm?
- Listen for the bass drum (turn up the bass frequency on the amp) and the cymbals / snare / any other percussion.
- Try playing the beat on a table, or on your own percussion.
- Is there a drum loop?

Melody shape
- What is the range of the song?
- Where is the highest vocal point in the melody, and is it significant (for instance, as an emotional climax)?
- Draw the graphic shape of the melody.
- Does it have a bold architectural shape or is it harmony driven?
- Are there any other moments when the melody specifically reflects/colours the words?

Arrangement
- List the instruments that you can hear.
- Where do the changes in instrumentation happen- for what reasons?
- Is there anything very particular or surprising about this song's orchestration?
- Are there any call-and-response moments?

Harmony
- When do the chords change—listen and clap on the changes.
- Work out and sing the bass line.
- Are there any surprises?
- Is the chord sequence different, or similar to another song you know?

Lyrical Features
- Write out the words, identify any rhymes.
- Is there a narrative? Does it contain any particular gritty details?
- Are there any cultural references that make the song more authentic or specific?

Melody

What survives every change in system is melody.
Igor Stravinsky

Working in theatre and composing songs, poet and songwriter Boris Howarth told me to test a song by removing the backing (harmony or instrumentation) and singing the song by itself. In Howarth's view, 'the melody needs to be able to work on its own if you want it to have the most powerful effect. The backing then assists and supports and gives extra depth.' Melodies exist in every culture and because we are vocal creatures each culture has developed its own style of singing and melodic composition. Wherever you go there seem to be certain universal shapes. How far do you recognise the following generalisations, for instance?

- sad melodies fall
- jumpy melodies excite
- smooth melodies calm
- extremities of pitch are exciting
- a monotone draws you in
- the minor third is the most soothing interval.

Melodic shapes can be seen as a series of hills and valleys and if you look at traditional notation they are very visible. Take a melody you know well and try and draw its shape, noticing how it moves, repeats and changes. Consider the shape of the melody, the roll and movement in pitch and rhythm, the potential for dynamics, the inflection and colouration of the words. Listen to the story of the song and listen to the shape of the lines. Here are some games with melody, which I have found can work well in terms of demystifying what melody is and how it operates.

- **Take a simple nursery rhyme.**
Draw its shape—try to do it freely without worrying too much about the details.
Try to get the overall shape, the big hills and valleys. Loosen up.

- **Take a sentence from a conversation.**
Repeat it out loud a number of times and draw the shape based on your speech inflection.
Repeat it now with the shape in mind and accentuate the pitch variety.

- **Take a four-line lyric.**
Take each line in turn and draw the shape from your speech inflection.
Look at the complete four-line melody shape and change it where necessary to make a better composition (for instance, if every line finishes with a downward swoop maybe change one, check how the melody shape reflects the words).

- **Take a lyric and try to find the natural rhythm of the word to a constant beat.**
Notate the accents with a line under the syllable.
Try reciting the lyric in a number of different rhythmic forms.
Decide which works best, which words want to shine out, which want space.

- **Take a dice and identify each number with a note on a keyboard – either every semitone or the white notes or a set of notes from a mode.**
Throw eight times and write down the numbers.
Play your melody with no rhythm.
Add a pulse and try again creating a more 'dynamic' melody.

An exercise I use for exploring and understanding group melody

When creating a group song I often make the melody before looking at the harmonic feel because in this way everyone can take an equal part and can feel a sense of ownership. The melody is created from speech inflection, the notes are chosen in a random fashion and everyone sees the melody growing. Sometimes the results are quite strange musically but the melody can be regularised into a particular style afterwards. If as an accomplished musician you start by playing a chord sequence and then making a melody on top you take away many people's ability to contribute. I have found that the following three-point process should work to include everyone.

Take a four-line lyric.
Discover the beat and pulse of the melody.
Through repetition and listening draw the shapes of the phrases on a black or whiteboard.
Use individuals' speech patterns to determine the shapes of the lines.
Repeat them so that everyone becomes familiar with the feel of the melody.

Ask for five numbers between 1 and 12 (explain that each number represents a certain note on a keyboard).
Familiarise the group with the five notes by using a series of call-and-response phrases.
Decide which one is the 'home' note, the resting place, the tonic.

Ask for the number of the first note in the first phrase of the melody.
Using this as the starting point follow the melody shape up and down attaching notes to points of the melody.
Follow this through phrase by phrase.
Offer alternate versions of each phrase and let group member decide which they like best. But don't force it—make it singable and interesting.

As you go along notate the melody numbers on the shape written on the board both so that you can remember and the group can see how the piece is developing. When it is finished you can then start to set it within a musical style and language and to add instruments, chords, or lyrics as required.

7

Song structure

Songs come in all shapes and sizes but when you start to take them apart there are certain basic building blocks to work with. It may not be necessary always to use each (in fact, such a song may sound mechanical or formulaic), but they all have different functions, and it is important to be able to recognise, explain and introduce each where necessary.

Introduction

This sets the scene, creates the mood, the background to the story, the musical style, the sense of place. It can be just music, just words, or a mix of the two. It can be extended or very short. The introductions are often missed out when we hear songs nowadays. For instance, the long rambles before Fats Waller jazz standards are rarely broadcast as part of the recording, while most operatic arias appear in concert without their recitative. We are in danger of throwing away valuable musical parts here!

Verse

Often tells a sequential story with a series of linked incidents or the progression of a single journey. Musically and lyrically, verses usually repeat the same structure each time with minor alterations of melody or rhythm.

Middle Eight

This is a term that has grown with a particular genre of popular music and jazz and has more to do with a harmonic structure than a lyrical one. It can often be just the third line of a verse.

Chorus

'The bit that keeps coming back', the repeated musical phrase that encapsulates the general sense and emotion of the song. The essence of the feeling behind the story. The chorus usually also contains the 'hook', the key melodic phrase that sticks in your mind. Wilfred Mellor wrote that the hook in a Beatles song 'will swing out of nowhere, catch you and grab you and make you remember that song!'

Refrain

It may not always be easy or possible to distinguish a refrain from a chorus, but the refrain is usually a one-line addition to a verse that serves the same purpose as the chorus in giving the universal truth of the song. It has a different structural position.

Bridge

Exactly as it says the bridge links between two parts of a song. It can be purely musical or it can make a lyrical journey too. The bridge marks the progression from one moment to the next and can have a transforming effect.

Instrumental

A moment to breathe, to let the emotion of a song settle in and progress without specific images. It can be written out in detail or left to a soloist to fly on the moment. (In 'Blue cotton', a song written with Adrian Mitchell about a woman in South Africa who loses her man in a car accident, the anger is only ever expressed through the solo, while the words just paint the picture).

Coda

The opposite to the Introduction, this ties up the song, resolves any issues both lyrically and musically and leaves you in a particular emotional state.

Most styles of songs have basic structures that exist in their genre and are open to small re-interpretations and adjustments. For example, a classic 'pop' song will have a short instrumental introduction, two verses, a bridge, a chorus, a verse, short instrumental, chorus and short coda—all fitting into a precise three-and-a-half minutes. However when you make a song use all of the elements above in whatever structure is appropriate. Let the story of the song determine the structure and only use an existing pattern only if it works for the song you are making.

7

Avoiding, using, subverting clichés

A cliché may be a phrase or image that has lost its original effectiveness or power from overuse, yet in songwriting it may be possible to turn the unoriginal into the original. Adrian Mitchell has been a key collaborator for over twenty years. After the first songmaking session we ran together I asked him what the key aspects of his sessions were. He said that they were finding the beat to your lyric, looking for details and images, telling stories and avoiding cliché. Mitchell wrote to me with the following advice:

Don't give me no silver moons, green grass or endless devotion. Let's hear it for green devotion, endless grass and the spittle-covered moon.

A cliché can be musical or lyrical, but if you have heard it before why use it? In a songmaking session people often first come up with ideas copied from their favourite star, melodic phrases that sound like a recent song, chord sequences that imitate. The only way to challenge it is to ask for originality and point out that the use of a cliché can take away the power of their song. How do you suggest those changes without offending someone, or squashing their enthusiasm? Mitchell's answer is to search for detail. Instead of singing about 'endless love' give a description of a jacket that they wore, a story of a journey together. Instead of singing about 'feeling so low' go round the block and describe in detail everything you see and what it makes you feel. Look for resonant images that are personal to you and your story and avoid the global clichéd emotional splurge. I am also grateful to and inspired by a set of ideas and games with lyrics produced by community musician Mary Keith, who has a formal music education background, went on to work with Community Music East in Norwich, and has worked often with MMM. Keith provides some great ways into songs lyrics here, offering creative ways of generating and expanding on lyrics. They are particularly effective in group workshops.

1. Begin with an idea or a subject word—as an example, we can use

FUTURE.

2. Words from a word: how many new words can you make up from your idea word?

3. Soundalikes: words that sound like your idea word (these can be made up).

4. Metaphors can work well, if your idea word was a colour, a smell, a taste …

5. Standpoints: what would it be like for someone else? Change the perspective to change the lyric.

6. Sonic starting points: use a piece of music and brainstorm the ideas it brings into peoples' heads, the more imaginative the better.

7. Haiku: employ this traditional poetic form of strictly seventeen syllables to sum up the essence of your idea.

8. Consequences: one person writes a line, next person adds one …

9. Nonsense words: look at examples of Dadaist poetry, Gaelic Mouth Music, foreign languages (careful!), onomatopoeia, alliteration, Scat singing, and so on.

10. Random/chance procedures: tear up pages from news papers, etc (think of David Bowie using William Burroughs 'cut-up' technique to produce some of his early lyrics).

11. Word Wizard: remove all the words in the world, but allow everyone to keep four of them. Find a partner, add your words together and write with just those words.

These ideas from Adrian Mitchell and Mary Keith address some of the problems associated with clichés in lyrics but with music it can be even more difficult. After all, some musical forms are effectively extremely formulaic, even clichéd—think of the very tight and limited 12-bar structure and progression of the blues, for example. In the previous section about melody I have tried to give a few ways to create original shapes and melodic phrases that are not likely to be derivative. Every lyric ought to suggest a unique melody and as you work on a song that individuality should flower. With harmony, chords and rhythm the choices again should be enormous. However we tend to use just a very few harmonic progressions (chord sequences) and this is where songs often fall into 'pastiche', into a copy of a style and a feel. Again, musical clichés need to be avoided, or subverted, or remixed into something different.

Some themes for songmaking, and short stories about MMM songs

Here are some of the themes and stories from MMM songmaking projects over the last few years. I offer them as glimpses into worlds made possible by song, as examples of the kinds of music we have been lucky enough to help to make. Sometimes we have facilitated it with considered deliberation, other times it's just kind of happened, songs as happy—even if they are sad—accidental inspirations. It helps so much to have a theme or a real context for a song and if you are working over a period of time it means that there is some sense of thematic unity to a set of songs. At MMM we have made space for creative songmaking with people of all ages and skills. The essence of our approach has been to search for detail by making the songs relate closely to peoples' lives and to what they know best.

Morecambe Streets

Everyone knows something about where they live, and we all have thoughts or memories about our surroundings.

> 1. Think about your house, flat, room, tent.
>
> 2. Choose one item or aspect of that place and write it down (or tell it to someone who does the writing).
>
> 3. Ask questions about it—its location, colour, shape, your attitude towards it, from where, owned by, its purpose, other things the same.
>
> 4. Look for interesting phrases that show your personal way of speaking or communicating—underline them.
>
> 5. Re-arrange the words and phrases, put them together into groupings, start to edit out bits you do not like, start to develop a beat to the words.

At MMM we used this basic process over four years to work with adults and children and create over 450 songs and poems. The variety was immense and the amount of deep emotion and truthful content truly inspiring. It was a point where the social work aspects of community music were at their foremost with a large amount of soul-searching and truth-telling that invested some of the songs with great power. Some of the songs have also proved timeless and universal enough to be performed in a number of different circumstances since the project finished. Some of them were so personal that they could not transfer at all—they worked best for the individual person as a way of reflection. The music for each was composed collaboratively with each songmaker so the variety of style is enormous. Most of the songs fit into a clear genre that reflects the person's taste and the lyric. Some people contributed more to the musical process than others but the songs were always made by the songwriter and the individual. They could never have arisen out of thin air and the combined creative energy meant that the songs were owned by both people. Here are very brief descriptions of half-a-dozen of the songs from the Morecambe Streets project.

'**Black bags**'—a comic music hall style song that catalogues the steady growth of the black bags in a back alley over a week written by an older woman who was fed up with the council for not removing them.

'**Under the stairs**'—a rhythmically delivered fantasy about the terrible world hidden in an under the stairs cupboard written with a group of 12-13 year olds.

'**Mat Meyer**'—a rap about a lad, his house, pets and family.

'**My bike**'—a tiny song about a bike kept in a loo.

'**McDevitt's light**'—an old-time waltz as an elegy to a security light that transformed the life of a partially sighted older woman.

'**Black as the night**'—a song about a teenager's bedroom, what happened there and what she wanted to do with it!

Starting points for songs about homes

Journey through a house
An estate agent's four-line description
A foot square of wall paper
Five kinds of chair
Worst-smelling spot
A line of the song for each step on the stairs
Different people's approach to the stairway
A view from a window
Ghosts in your house
Vitriolic attack on...
House as a menu / a feast
Name the rooms
Flatter the house
Recite its duties
Describe it as a jailor / waiter
What if...
The house number as a starting point
The garden / garden shed
Dream houses
The viewpoint of the doormat / the front door
Street corner
Graffiti.

Start Again and Safety Net

In December 1998 MMM celebrated the 50th anniversary of the Universal Declaration of Human Rights with the start of a series of performances of *Start Again*, a choral song cycle by myself and the poet Adrian Mitchell. In a number of cities we recruited an adult's and a children's choir over the six weeks before the performance, then brought in a band and two professional soloists for rehearsals and performance on the day. The context for the piece was real and I am convinced that people sang with clearer voice and vision because they believed in the words that they were singing. Musically it crossed a number of genres but was unified by a series of melodic and harmonic developments. As with many of my larger compositions it used a classical structure and form but a vernacular style of music which made it accessible to the widest possible audience.

After performances in Manchester, Morecambe, London, Gateshead, Ulverston, Hebden Bridge and Lancaster we realised the possibility of using the theme to do new creative work with people. This particularly focused on our projects with people with special needs in a number of different centres where we used the theme to look at very personal reflections on the global laws. For people whose worlds are generally quite small and 'self-centred' it was interesting to bring a sense of the greater outside world and the similar problems that affect people across the world.

Right Number 22

Every member of a society has the right to a safety net that will provide the money and status necessary for them to enjoy a dignified life in their society.

1. Choose three aspects of your life that create a safety net for you - these can be people, objects, places, things you do....

2. Write down a few lines about each.

3. Think about the way that they help you to survive and live a fulfilling life and craft a short phrase that expresses this.

4. Develop that phrase into a two or four line chorus.

5. Develop the three aspects into small stories that are in effect verses for your song.

6. Consider the whole and add a bridge, an intro, a coda or whatever else makes this a satisfying lyric.

Safety Net became the title for all of this work and here are very brief descriptions of four of the songs from the project.

• **'I've got a voice'**—written at a college for students with cerebral palsy this song considered their difficulties with the physicality of speech and the problems that people in other countries have with getting their voice heard for political reasons.
• **'Appearance'**—written at a secondary school where students felt victimised because of the way they looked and because of their history and reputation.
• **'Makes me feel sad'**—written at a school about the bullying and 'torture' that goes on in the playground.
• **'Private thoughts'**—written at a house for people with mental health problems and singing about the fact that you don't always have to tell people what you are feeling, you have the right to your own private thoughts.

Starting points for songs about human rights

Use these to try and find individual stories:
What is a human right?
What are your human rights?
Why do we have these rights?
Who breaks your human rights?
How do you deal with conflicting rights?
Rights in relationships, rights of independence, rights of social behaviour.
How can we fight for our rights?
How can we deal with people who abuse the rights?
Write some new rights!
Not Rights …what is not right?

Finally, two other short stories about songs and their making

'Loyal fan'

Songmaking in a youth club. The theme of songs about where we live, with a group of sceptical guitar-playing lads, whose musical enthusiasms are Oasis and Stone Roses. The conversation is transcribed loosely on to pieces of paper. There are questions about the house, the room, the details of the room, attachments and lateral thoughts. We look at the scribbles and pick out one thing to investigate more: the Stone Roses poster on the wall. We choose this because it relates to the love of music and there is a fantastic image of a guitar hanging in front of the poster gathering the band's energy by osmosis. Then there are other questions we are curious about: 'Where did you get it ... when ... where exactly is it ... what does it look like ... what do the band mean to you?' The lyric takes a couple of weeks to flesh out and it takes over a month to complete musically and arrange with the band. The tune and chords come from exploring the kind of typical Manchester genre of rhythmic feel and harmony, trying to find music that is not too obviously clichéd, that is the right pitch for the singer, and looking for a hook that will help us remember the song.

It's a bit of paper, be annoyed if I lost it,
given by my brother 2 years ago
Above my bed I look up at it,
collage of colours swimming in paint

I never saw them, my second favourite band
Ian Brown's voice made me a loyal fan
I never thought that they'd split
When they did I said shit
I'll never see them, I never saw them, Oh Damn

I hang my guitar and it covers the poster,
involves them in my music
Want a sound like them, a sound like Oasis,
want their influence inside of me

I never saw them …

'Ask me'

Songmaking with a group of eight children in a school for children with severe and complex disabilities. We are investigating human rights and our relationship to the world, trying to understand the global rules by finding equivalent situations within our own lives. The Right to Privacy is right number 12 of the Universal Declaration of Human Rights, and we talk about those aspects of our lives that we want to keep private and what we feel about them. A number of key issues arise and become the heart of a short song. The tune comes from choosing numbers (that relate to notes on an Appalachian dulcimer) and attaching them to words; it is a simple tune with a lovely call-and-response moment that develops in the second verse. I add the chord sequence at that moment with a reggae feel that seems right for the rhythms of the words, and the song goes on to be performed in many situations. These are personal stories with universal resonances and a simple effective melody and feel.

Nobody look in my secret diary.
Ask me. Ask me
Please can I come into your bedroom.
Ask me. Ask me

It's my book
It's my space
It's my special time on my own

Ask me nicely and you can hold my hand.
Thank you. Thank you
Ask me nicely and you can sing my song.
Thank you. Thank you

It's my hand
It's my song
It's my special time on my own.

INSPIRATION

Imagination has a fingerprint
Each dream is a new template
Each emotion has contours
Add inspiration and create.

You say this is too far away
This is not in your command
It is! Inspiration is as close to you
As the fingers on your hand.

chapter 8

New technologies and music-making

by Rachel Healey

8

The heart of my set-up is my laptop and US428 Soundcard. Everything connects via this. The three main software packages I use are Propellerheads' Reason and Recycle, and Cubase SX. This set-up is a full recording studio with instruments, samplers, loop players, mixing desks and effects units. The three programmes link up and with little tutoring of the basics people can soon be creating their own music. The Laptop is a two-gig Pentium 4 with 512-meg RAM. The s o u n d c a r d is a Tascam US428. I then connect various bits of equipment up to this set-up, including synths, samplers and external effects. I also use Soundbeam.

Heidi Manning, tutor in music technology at Manchester College of Arts and Technology

95% of technical problems can be solved by applying the ancient mantra, 'Is it plugged in? Is it switched on?"

Workshop leaders Dave Camlin and Mark Newport

The musical cultures prevalent in Britain contain judgements about how to make music and how not to, what it should sound like, who is qualified to do it, when and where it should be done. It is my view that the increasing use of new technologies can break down these judgements and make music more accessible as well as more present in every aspect of our lives and society. Most community musicians believe that everyone can make music. I believe that new technologies open it up further, making composition even more accessible to anyone, including people who have severe motor or sensory impairment. New technologies can also affect how we listen (to the world), and what we do with the sounds we notice. As a result of new technologies, there is almost constantly music around us. Perhaps most importantly, the more that people are involved in music-making, the more choices we have about our relationship with music.

There is no doubt that the use of new technologies is engaging greater numbers of people in music of all kinds. As Anthony Everitt writes about the impact of the digital revolution, in *Joining In: An Investigation into Participatory Music*, 'Musical democrats should cheer'. In this chapter I want to look at digital developments in three indicative areas of particular relevance to community musicians: working with young people in the production of contemporary pop sounds, with special needs groups, and in projects that work towards the creation of sound installations.

One useful starting definition of what we mean by 'music' is 'organised sound': someone is making music if they are making decisions about where to place sounds in relation to other sounds or silence. These sounds could be notes played on a guitar, spoken words, synthesised beats, or the drop of a pin. We could combine them in real time, by getting a group of musicians together in a room. But with new technologies, we can store sounds and then play around with the order at our leisure. We may aspire to write the greatest club anthem of all time, or we may be musically inspired by the crunch of autumn leaves. New technologies allow us to capture and manipulate sound much like a digital visual artist takes a picture and manipulates it using a software package like Photoshop. Anything we can hear with our ears, and some things we can't, are available for us to weave into musical compositions.

Why use new technologies? New technologies can allow the easy manipulation of sound by anyone regardless of what we might think of as traditional musical training. We can record our own voices or favourite sounds and use them as the basis for a piece of music. We can change the source sounds: bend pitches, add reverberation, or echo. We can display stored sounds graphically as little boxes, and then play around with the order of the boxes (which is much less cumbersome than splicing reel-to-reel tape). We can start with a pre-set rhythm track and bass track, and compose our own rap or vocal melody to sing over the top. Using techniques such as these, anyone can compose music: choosing sounds that you like, and arranging them in an order that you like. New technologies can also encourage us to listen more. Amplification can draw attention to sounds we may not notice. We can easily record and play back sounds in our environment, whether they occur naturally, or we make them ourselves, and listen to them again and again. When we have heard the sound a snail makes, this may change our view of snails, forever. This is a primary motivation for sound artist and educator Duncan Chapman. As he says, new technologies can give 'access to a whole range of sound worlds that are hard to reach by other means. Also, they provide the ability to have a change of scale—to turn a small gesture into a large gesture. Something very tentative and very small can become something very significant. It's a bit like having a magnifying glass.'

8

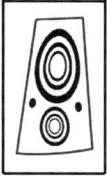

The technologies are the tools. Like any instrument, the skill and creativity of the player or operator, as well as their purpose, are what produce the end result. It is important not to lose sight of this simple fact, as learning about the technology for its own sake frequently obscures the aim of making music. Musician and sound recordist Peter Cusack confirms this view in his own work. He told me: 'Although I use new technologies all the time they are not the aim. The project's focus is to create a piece for a performance, or to explore the sounds of the environment in a creative context, or to make a radio programme. The technologies are the means to that end. Duncan Chapman goes further: 'I don't think the technology is separate from the music'. He even stated to me that he 'hate[s] the phrase "music technology"', which in his view suggests a spurious relationship. Technology can be human, can be old-fashioned—one of Chapman's favourite pieces of equipment is 'my own ears'. Sometimes new technologies are imbued with a kind of cultural reverence, though: it is the view of DJ and community musician Sean Canty that community musicians 'need to be at the cutting edge of music. Dance music and hip-hop are the biggest selling musics around and we need to be at the forefront as leaders not followers'. For Canty, new technologies can open up a level of acceptance and generate enthusiasm in workshops, particularly with young people, because they are associated with the soundtrack of the contemporary. This has been the experience of Heidi Manning as well:

If I went into a young offenders' centre with my guitar and said 'OK let's make some tunes', I can't see the young people feeling stimulated and willing to contribute. If I went in, with an array of music technology equipment and started to play a hip-hop beat and got people to create some tracks and lyrics to rap to, I would have much more interest. This is the type of music that most young people listen to and this is the type of music that they are stimulated by and want to create. It can be a way to gain the group's enthusiasm and trust, and respect even, maybe.

On the practical side, new technologies offer the community musician:

- the ability to be cool: to make music that sounds like current pop and underground music, which also helps get the attention of specific groups, such as in prison or youth groups

- alternative ways of helping people listen to and make music, with ease of access and facility for people who may not be, for whatever reasons, physically or technically proficient in conventional musical ways

- a flexible tool to do useful things, such as make multiple copies of music produced during workshops, fast and of good quality

- access to new sound worlds, that can expand the musical imagination of participants, like recording underwater, or amplifying very quiet sounds

- access to sounds not normally readily available in most workshop settings, like pre-recorded samples of a Steinway piano or a green parrot, or big band horn section

- a means of capturing and manipulating sounds, such as recording speech or other vocal noises and playing them backwards

- a wonderful capacity to store sounds—on CD, MP3s, wav files, minidisc, and so on

- ways of creating soundscapes. Anything from an installation on the theme of steam trains to transforming a classroom into a tropical rainforest

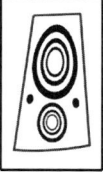

So, while new technologies open up possibilities in music that can make it more fun, accessible, and enriching, there are also pitfalls and limitations. These include:

- sampling may offer a poor approximation of acoustic instruments

- if replacing 'live' musicians, the importance of interaction, of the potential for musical dialogue can be lost (and for many people this is the whole point of making music)—while the impact of the live performance can be dissipated

- more generally, the solo focus (on a computer terminal or screen, for instance) can be profoundly atomising in workshops. This is particularly important as community music is usually about fostering a sense of community, after all

- 'toys for the boys'—there can be issues around gender exclusion

The biggest danger is using technologies (often unwittingly) in ways that limit creativity and reinforce unhelpful notions of what music should sound like. Paul Wright, former education director of Sonic Arts Network, chooses workshop leaders very carefully: 'amongst all the artists I have worked alongside in the past 13 years, and literally hundreds of hours of observing workshops, I can only think of perhaps three or four who can really do it. That's because the workshop skills required are a considerable craft, developed over years by gifted individuals.'

Some techno stuff, and contemporary youth sounds

When you record and play back music, the equipment and technology you use inevitably affects it. Some people argue that you will never get the same 'feel' with digital sound as with analogue sound—that magnetic tape recordings and vinyl records, or valve radios, for instance, have a 'warmer' sound. This is because all digital sound relies on on/off commands, on however minute a scale, so that, effectively, the sound has been chopped into tiny fragments, which the brain experiences even if we cannot necessarily perceive it con-

sciously. Sound is affected at every step of the recording, storing and playing back process. So the microphone you use, the types of cable, input sockets, storage media, number of copies, and speakers may all affect the end result. But digital does not decay in anything like the same degree as earlier recording technologies—the fiftieth digital copy of a workshop recording will sound pretty much like the first. Nor, of course, is there chewed tape or scratched vinyl to worry about. For capturing and storing sounds, digital technology really can assist the community musician in important ways.

A number of digital forms have been made commercially available in the past two decades for recording and storing music. CDs are easy to handle, to write on, and most people have playback equipment for them. You can make a CD using a computer-based CD recorder, or a freestanding CD recorder.

DAT (digital audio tape) is probably the favoured medium for sound recordists, ethnomusicologists, and some journalists. DAT consists of tiny equipment that will fit easily into your kit bag, and recordings are of good quality and durability.

Minidisc is a common digital medium in community music and with sound artists, because of its portability relative to its quality. Using a good microphone, most minidisc recordings sound good, and it is possible to do a limited amount of editing using the minidisc recorder itself.

MP3 is music technology for mobile phone ringtones and especially for sourcing music from the Internet, such as from music-sharing websites like Napster and more recent official industry ones. Both minidisc and MP3 employ compression: to reduce the size of music files information that the human ear does not usually notice is discarded. This leaves a much smaller bundle of digital information, which can be stored and moved around more easily.

Ringtones are a newer public/personal music experience, which you can download, personalise, or record or compose your own. There are new opportunities here for community musicians, I am sure of it!

Midi (Musical Instrument Digital Interface) technology needs a mention here. It has been around since the 1980s, and is widely used in community music, by composers, and in the music industry.

8

The main use of midi is that it enables electronic instruments from any manufacturer to communicate with one another and with a computer. Midi files are a sequence of instructions to play specified notes at a specified pitch and for a specific duration, a bit like an electronic musical score. Midi files do not contain any sample data (that is, sound)—you play them using your own instrument (such as digital piano, drum samples, midi guitar), or your own collection of samples. Midi instruments are a collection of switches, sounds already programmed in. For example, a midi guitar plays sampled guitar sounds. It will interpret a midi file using these guitar sounds. The instrument might contain other switches to manipulate the sound: volume, pitch, pan, and so on. Midi files are small because they do not contain any sound, and versatile because you can change tempo and pitch in real time; on the down side they obviously do not sound as good as a full rendition using the original instruments.

The laptop computer has become a tremendous asset as a mobile recording studio for community musicians. A decent hardware studio set-up, including a 38 track mixing desk, samplers, synthesisers, sound processors and recording equipment is very expensive specialist equipment. A good quality laptop, with a sound card, suitable music software and plug-ins (for effects like reverb), is massively cheaper. Because of its size and ease of portability, too, the laptop as a studio is important for working in the community. Duncan Chapman exploits these features in his work. 'I have a laptop, a single effects unit, a tiny mixing desk, and a stereo microphone. I can almost fit my whole kit into my hand luggage. And I can make a CD for the people I'm working with and give it to them at the end of the workshop.' The kinds of software available give a sense of the kinds of ways you can make use of a laptop in music making.

Audiomulch: can be downloaded free for 90 days to make your own squelchy techno. It contains prepared samples so you can have fun playing around with the order and add effects and filters.

Cakewalk, Sibelius: both are notation software.

Cubase, Protools: multi-track sequencing and sound editing software.

Emagic Logic: for composition using synthesised sounds or your own audio and midi plug-ins, sound editing, notation, remixing.

Propellerheads: full studio set-up, including synthesizers, samplers, mixer, drum machine, effects, and a sample library of orchestral sounds. Midi interface. Add-ons include ReCycle (an enhanced loop player and editor), and ReBirth (a collection of synthesisers and drum machines for making authentic sounding techno music).

In order to make a CD of your music, you need to make all of the separate tracks into a stereo master recording (you might have separate tracks for vocal, guitar, drums and bass line, for instance). If you are using software like Cubase, once you have worked on your music, got each track exactly as you want it, you can mix down the whole piece into one audio file by clicking just one button. There is no quality loss or fiddling with plugs and wires. One advantage of having effects (like reverb, compression, echo, pitch bend) on your laptop is that you can have one sound process on as many channels as you wish. So you could plug in three microphones, a record deck, a drum machine and other instruments, and have reverb on all of them. To achieve this in a hardware studio, you would need to connect a reverb unit to each channel.

What can be lost with using a laptop for recording is the image and experience of a more traditional studio that still attract many people in the first place. As DJ and studio technician Tray C puts it, 'I just love the feeling of sitting down behind a mixing desk the size of a sofa'. The old buzz of plugging in the leads, coiling up cable, sticking everything down with gaffer tape, just does not translate when the laptop you are now using could just as well be being used for updating the financial accounts, or writing a student essay. The romance of the recording studio resides in odd places, like the buttons and sliders on the desk. Musician and studio engineer Rob Overseer told me that, 'when it comes to minute adjustments, there's nothing as good as a slider that goes up and down, or an EQ knob. People like k n o b s . ' There may be a wider point here for many who are interested in popular music: many bands, for instance, want acoustic 'authenticity', and may positively distrust the digital revolution for its role in 'diluting' the meaning of music.

The main disadvantage of the laptop for community musicians is that, like every computer, it is predicated on one individual's needs and activity. Community music usually works on a consensual, group-oriented model. One way to address this problem can be to project the screen, using a data projector or large plasma screen. Then more people can see what is displayed without having a crowd of bodies around one little laptop. But, whether because of limits of design, time, patience, interest, or physical abilities, the laptop may run counter to the principles of involvement, inclusivity, and working together. It is a useful tool as part of a whole set up, but can never replace having several means of controlling sound. Paul Crawford, Drake Music Project senior tutor, puts it this way:

I see the computer as one instrument capable of doing lots of different things. Because it's a scarce resource, we think that everyone needs to get their fair share. But instead we can just treat it as one more instrument to be played by one or two people.

New technologies have opened up other fields of music-making too. Perhaps the best known of these, due to the global spread of rap, hip hop and dance music in recent years, is the whole cluster of work around DJ-ing, beat matching, scratching and sampling. An accomplished DJ spinning and mixing records is playing an instrument requiring skill and years of practice. In my view it is as technically complex as a conventional instrument. The basic kit is two record players with pitch control, a mixer with a cross fader so you can blend the sound of each record with the other, headphones that block out external noise, and the option of a sampler built in to the mixer. Some DJs also add their own vocals to their music via a microphone, often as part of a headset, plugged in to the mixer. Hip-hop DJs were the first to employ scratching, which is increasingly used by DJs in all musical genres. Scratching is basically using the sounds on the records as raw material for creating improvised music, usually percussive. The DJ plays the record like an instrument, using faders to further control the sound. A scratch sequence may last a few seconds, or several minutes.

Any sound can be sampled using a microphone and a device to store sounds, such as a minidisc recorder, tape recorder, hard disk recorder, or a sampler. Samples of pre-existing music are among the most popular: the screams and grunts of soul singer James Brown are supposed to be among the most sampled pieces of music in contemporary pop. Once you have your sample, what is then done with this sound is up to you. For instance, once the sound is stored in the sampler (a real one or using sampling software on a computer), it can be manipulated in various ways, such as being looped, played backwards, or having the end chopped off. Samplers built into a mixer can capture a few seconds of a track and play it back at the touch of a button. The DJ can create a little riff to play at will, or a loop which goes on and on. This can add an extra layer of sound to the whole mix. If the playback device is attached to a sound processor (effects unit), processes can be added to alter the sound such as echo, reverberation, or changing the pitch. If it is attached to a midi instrument the sample can be triggered using the midi switches. One sample could be triggered to play at different pitches, or a different sample could be attached to each switch.

As evidence of the relentless onward drive of the digital revolution, you can now get CD players with pitch control, and an interface allowing manipulation of the CD for scratching. One version features plastic platters on top, which you can manipulate like a pair of old-fashioned records. You can even put a pair of 7" singles on top if you desire the feel and nostalgic appeal of vinyl. According to Sean Canty, DJ and project worker for Dhamak (a fusion project based in East Lancashire, incorporating rapping, dhol drums and DJs), such digital developments, 'are near enough as good as record decks for mixing and scratching. I'm all for them. They're great for community music projects because the kids can write a track using Reason, burn it onto a CD, then DJ with it straight away.' Synthesised sounds and sound processes are a major element of the music most DJs play. Many community music projects offering DJ skills training also offer training in creating your own music, and some of the skills overlap. Software packages like Reason and Cubase enables the creation of hip-hop, dance and jungle music, and can offer sounds that are impossible to create using conventional instruments.

8

As a central part of their social agenda, the London-based ragga/jungle band Asian Dub Foundation established an education wing, AFDED, in 1998. AFDED merges contemporary pop awareness and style with music technology, a community music ethos with an overtly political commitment. I asked AFDED's Sonia Mehta about the organisation, and its choice and application of technology.

ADFED offers project-specific music technology courses covering sampling, rhythm programming, sequencing, editing, writing and arranging songs, mixing and mastering, and incorporating traditional instruments. Each course ends with a showcasing event, and every participant leaves with a CD of his or her own music. We target young people passionate about making music, and especially those who don't have access to musical equipment and training. We also focus on issues around ethnic minority youth cultures, social exclusion, gender imbalance, and refugee/asylum issues.

The technology the organisation is currently using is the MPC 2000XL. We find that this is an excellent introductory tool for young people coming in at entry level and for those who have never been in a studio environment before. It gives them a hands-on approach to producing music from start to finish and to a professional standard.

ADF member Dr Das developed his teaching practice using the MPC during his time as a tutor at Community Music, London. He found that it was relatively affordable, gave students a hands-on approach to music making, and helped to develop a style of music that was unique and exciting for its time. While it is a sampling kit essentially, it reached beyond the depths of electronic music and helped to fuse rhythm and melody in a way that was not possible before, certainly not through any hardware device. Although technology has surged ahead through the use of various software programmes, many hip-hop producers still favour the use of the MPC. The MPC is relatively cheaper than computer-based software and is an all-in-one tool for making music. It also has the capacity to work alongside software applications, as well as encouraging hands-on musicality, as opposed to producing music by the click of a button.

Making music with people who have special needs

A lot of people I work with have a different perception of the world. It's very inspiring to us to understand a bit about that. Lots of reasons are given for doing music with people with special needs: increased sociability, and so on. But we have loads to gain from them, too.
Duncan Chapman

People with special needs frequently have experiences of d i s e m p o w-erment and discrimination, including around making aesthetic judgements and choosing what to listen to. Music workshops can offer an opportunity to move beyond this, with new technologies providing the means for people to make choices. It must be acknowledged that, while using specialist interfaces for people with limited physical movement can mean gaining some control versus having none, the subtleties normally available to an able-bodied person may be compromised. However, with innovative new controllers, and infinitely innovative workshop leaders, this is not necessarily the case, and we need to guard against going for simplicity at the expense of creativity. Ownership is a key concept here. 'The fundamental thing is the connection between the person and the thing they make,' says Chapman. 'My aim in all of my work is to get people to realise the world makes a noise, and they can have a connection with it and they can choose. Special needs children and in fact adults historically have not always had a choice, especially in music. So I focus on giving value to things people do already, and then we can frame those to create a piece of music. For example, with PMLD [profound and multiple learning difficulties] people, we can create pieces from their vocalisations.' I have seen Chapman at work in special needs schools, and the excitement in a girl's face when she listens and realises 'That's my voice!' is striking.

There are many projects aiming to involve disabled people in music making, and there is a general notion that technology somehow makes music more accessible. However, to use it sensitively and creatively requires much skill and experience. There is, after all, a complex cluster of issues involved, including cultural issues, empowerment, aesthetics, personal creativity, and the individual controlling his or her environment. I have seen performances where the limit of a disabled person's creative involvement is to switch a pre-recorded looped sample (recorded by someone else) on and off at pre-determined moments by moving their hand in and out of a Soundbeam (a midi device; see below). It looks impressive, but so much more is possible! One alternative is suggested by Paul Crawford: instead, the Soundbeam could be connected to a pitch bend sound process, which operates the live sampled sound of an instrument being played by another musician. Operating the switch remains the same simple task: moving in and out of the Soundbeam. But the decision-making regarding when to use it is musically very sophisticated. Soundbeams and other switches can also be used to control the overall volume of the whole piece, or to fade other players in and out.

Established by Adele Drake in 1988, the Drake Music Project is probably the best-known organisation making music involving new technologies with disabled people in Britain. With regional offices, it employs a core permanent staff including workshop leaders, and also employs freelancers to run projects. Each tutor has their own approach. Crawford, for instance, is a senior tutor, and it is his firm view that 'it's not therapy. It's about creating opportunities for people to create music in their community. We often work with disabled and non-disabled people in the same environment. And technology never defines what we are doing. If it can help to get the job done, great'. The Drake project's work is based around three areas: music, music technology, and access technology, which is about making computer environments useful and easy to use. It is involved in research and development of new tools for computer users with disabilities, including Soundbeam and the new E-scape sound editing software. In fact, accessing the technology is an important initial issue for many disabled people, and an area of significant activity for music-making projects , by Drake and others.

Peripherals, or ways of interacting with the information displayed on the screen, are conventionally limited to a computer keyboard, a mouse, and perhaps a piano-style midi keyboard. However, a range of other means has been developed to facilitate greater access to digital technology. The Soundbeam is perhaps the best known: it is a device that emits an infra-red beam, and when the beam is broken (for instance, by the physical movement of the body), it triggers a midi switch. It looks like a torch and can be clipped on to a microphone stand, wheelchair arm, or anywhere really. Other devices include tracker balls, joysticks, ergonomic keyboards, and touch sensitive pads—which can be activated by rolling a wheelchair over them, in turn triggering a midi switch, for instance. Nor is all access

technology necessarily high tech: it might be as simple as tilting a tabletop, providing a surround desktop, ensuring sturdy clips and balanced stands, for example.

In a contrasting approach, focussing on fun and getting fingers on buttons, Heidi Manning describes the material she developed while working with Drake for that vital first session:

I have programmed the samplers, MIDI creator and Soundbeam so that all the notes are of the same scale and fit together no matter what order they are played in. Then the group can focus on the playing of the music rather than the technicalities. When they have control of something that is sounding good and they are creating it, it builds up confidence and self-esteem. If they were playing something and it was all out of key they would feel as if they were doing something wrong and it would not be half as enjoyable.

This raises useful questions, including: from where do we get our notions of what sounds 'right' and 'wrong', and is it the community musician's role to make such decisions? Perhaps making music in a particular genre necessarily involves adopting set notions of what it should sound like. These are vital questions to consider when we aim to develop others' creativity, particularly with people who have learning disabilities. In identifying and addressing these kinds of issues, it is perhaps in special needs contexts that we all have the most to gain from new technologies.

Sound installations

Because of their ease of use, portability and high quality of reproduction, new technologies have had a significant impact on sound installations as a public form of artwork. Peter Cusack lectures in Sound Arts and Design at the London College of Communication. One of Cusack's key areas of activity is in 'environmental sound recording and acoustic ecology. I have a long interest in how people interact with everyday sounds on all levels, personally, socially and culturally and have been involved in projects in many contexts, educational, public art or completely on my own. An example is the Your Favourite London Sound project where many hundreds of Londoners have been asked what is their favourite London sound and why. It is an attempt to find out what Londoners think of their soundscape and the role sound plays in daily life. Outcomes have been CDs, exhibitions and radio programs plus a small involvement in discussions at the GLA on the development of London's Ambient Noise Strategy.' I asked Cusack about the practicalities of creating artwork that explores 'acoustic ecology', and he kindly provided me with Cusack's Five Step Plan to creating a sound installation:

1. Theme, location and context of the installation

What is the total budget? Factor all costs in, and be accurate.

Who will be making it?

Who will be experiencing it?

What are you hoping to communicate to them or elicit in them?

How long will it be up for?

Who is hosting it, and why?

What type of space—indoors/outdoors, big/ small, noisy/quiet, dead/reverberant acoustics?

What facilities are present? Is there electricity, lighting, toilets, etc?

Ease of access—lifts, steps, width of doorways, parking, trolleys, etc. You may have heavy or bulky equipment to move.

Does it require someone to look after it or switch it off and on? If so, who?

Are other provisions for security needed?

2. Structure of the installation

Will there be several different recordings or just one?

What format are you using for your recording(s)?

Can participants choose to control the sounds themselves?

How will the sounds be triggered? Soundbeams, pressure pads, switches ...

Will recordings be on continuous loops or just play once?

If using speakers, how many will you have? Do you want them to be obvious or hidden? Where will they be placed? Ceiling, floor, inside a sculpture...

If using headphones, how many will you have? Where?

Can equipment withstand the treatment it might receive from members of the public?

How much cable is needed? Mains, loudspeaker, audio, microphone.

How many plugs and sockets?

8

3. Recording equipment

Factors include quality, portability, ease of use, and cost.

The equipment you use depends on what you wish to record: human voices are straightforward, while underwater sounds, or a huge volume range, are more complex.

Minidisc plus a good quality microphone are a common choice.

4. Record your samples and create your installation

Do you need studio facilities for creating/editing/preparing the sound?

5. Set up your installation

Estimate accurately how long you will need for setting up and how much help will be required.

You will need spare equipment—especially cables, and gaffertape!

Consider whether you would like to make a record of the installation: a master recording, a sound recording or video of the event, interviews with participants, and so on.

Conclusion: sound advice

Using new technologies in community music-making can be rewarding and liberating. I hope I have shown a little of how they can also make music out of unconventional sounds, as well as help people who may not be able to work in conventional ways with instruments or their voices simply to make some music. I want to finish with some advice from three practitioners, each of whom I asked about 'any little tricks' they had devised that they could rely on in workshops.

Heidi Manning advises: 'Always have something prepared, even if it's just a few beats programmed as a starting point for people to work with. And have some effects ready: warming up with a new workshop group as if everyone was in space, in the jungle, on a desert island, can really break the ice.'

In Peter Cusack's view, 'most projects are unique and so new ideas have to be developed every time. But playing familiar sounds—speech, for instance—backwards generally gets a good response'.

Duncan Chapman suggests taking a 'sound journey': 'go on a journey (inside or outside), and collect digital recordings of five sounds that mean something to you. Then construct the session around composing something using those.'

Acknowledgements

Thanks to Morph, Rob Overseer, Ruth Boswell, Peter Cusack, Duncan Chapman, Paul Wright, Heidi Manning, Sonia Mehta, Paul Crawford, Steve Lewis, Sean Canty, Jill Rakusen, George McKay, Pete Moser and Peter Brown

THEY'RE LIKE YOUR BABIES

I couldn't see what had brought him here.
But the bags he carried below his eyes
Were heavy. He put them down beside himself
and prepared for the workshop. Never said a word.

He curled his arm around his paper on the desk
Like he was cradling and talking to a baby child
I heard the scratching of his pen and watched
As all that baggage started to shine. First it went purple
And then through the purple a white light broke through
And then gold, fluorescent gold. It became gold
—he was surrounded by stacks of gold.

A tale of two hats by David Price

OK, everyone, thanks a lot for coming, let's make a start.

We're going to do a quick warm-up.

I want you to sing how you got here, to the tune of Danny Boy.

What do you mean, you first?

Oh, all right then…

For twelve years I was a singer-songwriter in bands and, despite making a reasonable living, I eventually began to feel that: a) this was not a proper job for a grown-up, and b) there was more I could do with whatever musical skills I had. I didn't know quite what, but I enrolled on a performing arts degree course in Newcastle. The time I had for reflection and learning was unexpectedly gratifying, and a week after graduating I got a job with Community Arts Workshop, based in Manchester. This was 1985 and I vividly remember my first workshop (though I didn't know what a workshop was at that point). It involved making paper hats for under-5s—not with, because the kids were so bored at this point, we ended up making the hats for them. As I recall, we then started processing rather forlornly around an East Manchester housing estate. And it started raining. Somehow the actuality of the practice had fallen someway short of the radical political history lectures we had been given at college.

And I discovered I was rubbish at making hats.

At that time, you couldn't be a real community artist without carrying about your person a well-thumbed copy of Owen Kelly's *Community Art and the State: Storming the Citadels*. Twenty years after its publication, this still remains one of the few books written which puts forward a theoretical framework for community arts. Because of the rhetoric and radicalism running through Kelly's argument, I was often left with a sense of failure if my projects weren't enabling people to rise up against the twin ogres of capitalism and Thatcherism. It was only when I subsequently heard Kelly say that getting people away from the television for a couple of hours every week was an overtly political act, that I felt vindicated for all those song-writing workshops and endless clapping games.

As it happened, over the next eight years I ended up helping people make music in a number of local campaigns and controversies. Perhaps the most heated of these grew, ironically, out of the effects of Thatcher's poll tax on Manchester City Council. By now I was part of a wonderfully creative community arts team at the Abraham Moss Centre, which now faced closure as a result of the City Council's attempt to balance the books. Our response was to protest in the only way we knew how. In Stars Below, an unashamed piece of agit-prop theatre I devised with Gerri Moriarty, Jane Rogers and about 200 participants, there was a song which grew out of a series of personal stories triggered when we asked people what 'taking part' meant to them. Even now, I find the lyrics powerfully touching:

Seeds blown across dusty wastes,
We landed on fertile earth and we grew.
And if they put cement over the cracks,
Our growth, our flowering would not be missed
By anyone but us:
We have no voice beyond the one we've grown,
To sing this song.

Well, they still shut us down (can't win 'em all, I suppose), and I was redeployed in the local Further Education College and from there, helped set up the Liverpool Institute for Performing Arts. When I was planning the courses to run at what inevitably became known as 'Paul McCartney's Fame School', I was convinced of the need to create a vocational preparation for participatory music leaders.

There was initial resistance to this idea, since community music was not considered part of 'the industry'. I would, and did, beg to differ, and what has happened in the intervening ten years only strengthens the argument in seeing non-formal music-making as a legitimate part of the music industry. Investment in community music activities now runs into hundreds of millions of pounds a year and an increasing number of successful musical acts have emerged through this route, though this is never the primary reason for this work being funded.

There are not only more opportunities for this work, there is, as George McKay noted earlier, a wider than ever range of contexts within which workshops now take place. So it is inevitable that we are moving away from describing it as 'community' music (with a clear and distinctive ideology) to 'non-formal' music-making, which more realistically reflects the diffuse (some would say diluted) political rationale for encouraging participation.

As you might have guessed by now, I earn my living these days advocating and advising others on music strategies (the jump from community musician to consultant is not as big as you might think). Everywhere I go, I seem to hear the same thing: there is now a significant shortfall in the supply of high-quality workshop leaders needed in order to meet the demand. The shortage of good training means that more gigging musicians than ever are finding themselves also running workshops, often with precious little prior experience. You may be one of them, rummaging through this handbook thinking 'what on earth can I do with them this week?' If so, here's another exercise for you to try:

1. Put this book down

2. Ask yourself 'why am I doing this work?'

3. Don't pick it back up again until you have an answer that you're completely satisfied with.

[There will now be a short musical interlude]

So, how did you get on with the exercise? Who wants to go first?

As with most of the exercises within this book, there are no 'wrong' answers, but I would suggest that there are some which might mean that you may find workshop practice less fulfilling and more difficult than it should be. If, for example, your answer was 'because it keeps me going financially until I get more gigs' then you may have little affinity with the groups you find yourself working with, and therefore little curiosity about their preferred style of learning, or their long-term development. Or, another response could be 'to get the best possible musical results out of a group because I am passionate about the music I bring to them'—this is sometimes the motivation for genre-specific musicians. If so, you may regularly find yourself frustrated because the musical progress of the group is slow, and you may not discover their potential for other forms of musical development, or what they can learn from each other, or even how they care for, and support one another.

I need to stress that there is nothing intrinsically, or ethically, 'wrong' in either of the responses listed above. And almost any response is better than the blank stare I have often encountered when asking the question in a training session. If you really are still struggling with a value-list, here are extracts from one Jennie Hayes prepared following her interviews with community artists:

Participatory artists believe:

• in the transformative power of involvement in original artistic
  expression
• in the value of creativity in social and community development
• in providing opportunities to develop everyone's creative potential
• in active creative collaboration between artists and others
• in achieving the highest quality
• in the equal importance of artistic and social aspirations.

Participatory artists respect:

• the need to understand the importance of the political, social,
  cultural and economic context within which they are working
• the particular contribution people in communities make to the
  artistic process, in partnership with the artist.

Participatory artists endeavour:

- to develop imaginative, inspiring and meaningful arts work with people
- to set up inclusive frameworks for involvement in arts work
- to value cultural distinctiveness and cultural identity
- to support the potential for individual and group progression
- to continue to develop their own skills and art form practice.

As a set of reasons for getting into this work, and as a rough pen picture of the people who have described their practice here, it's pretty good. The contributors to this book may all have different approaches to their workshop technique, but I believe they would subscribe to almost all of these values—particularly the first set. Also, I have found that the longer people do this kind of work the more likely they are to shift away from teaching people how to play set musical patterns to a freer (albeit riskier) approach. Earlier, Steve Lewis described the moment when he made that decision, and I was privileged to be there when another fine percussionist, Paul Dear, walked into a room full of primary school children and for the first time worked with what they could bring to the process, rather than what he could ask them to play. It was like watching someone run off the edge of a cliff ... and then gloriously fly. The session had a dynamism I had not seen before, and the participants were palpably proud of the pieces they had created.

There is a song in Stephen Sondheim's *Sunday In The Park With Georges*, a musical about the pointillist painter Georges Seurat, when Seurat has become so absorbed in the detail of a hat in his 'Sunday On La Grande Jatte' painting that hours have gone by without him noticing. He sings of revelling in the magic of artistic creation (the painting of a hat on to a blank canvas). This image, for me, captures the everyday miracle which happens when we enable people to express themselves. Being able to bring something into existence which wasn't there before is perhaps the most profound thing a human being can do. The moment when people realise that you don't have to be born with the creativity gene—that every single one of us can make some kind of a hat—is an inspiring one. And the most rewarding thing anyone can do is help them discover it.

This book is packed full of ideas which can stimulate people's innate creativity. But sometimes we think we have to do more of the stimulation than is really necessary, as I learned from Colin Seddon, founder of Inner Sense Percussion Orchestra. The following exercise of Seddon's works in part because sometimes leading isn't as effective as 'allowing'.

Tremble Piece
You start by getting people to sit, eyes closed and in a circle, with a percussion instrument each. Ask them to make the fastest, quietest sound (hence the tremble) they can and then, in their own time, they should simply offer a rhythmic riff in response to what they hear. As people gradually enter, the piece changes shape and feel and there'll be times when the pulse and even time signature vary wildly. But stay with it, because more often than not, you end up with a set of patterns which can become grooves, building into melodic lines and even full-blown pieces, without the facilitator doing much of any - thing.

The exponential growth of non-formal music-making in Britain has attracted the interest of a much wider community of educators, internationally as well. Put simply, this stuff works and when doors to musical participation, hitherto closed by more formal kinds of tuition, suddenly open up through taking part in workshops, it's not hard to see why. In the USA, young people's opportunities for organised group music-making are still largely restricted to orchestra or marching bands. Compare this to even remote areas of Britain where, for example, one in three young Shetland Islanders plays music—in school, in rock bands, in traditional music sessions, Samba bands and so on. There are, by now, comparatively few schools in this country that have not had workshops run by visiting music leaders, and those working in more formal contexts—primary teachers, music teachers, music service instrumental tutors, even conservatoire tutors—are eager to introduce such practices into their own teaching styles. Despite this, the body of work which examines these approaches remains pitifully thin.

And yet, as welcome as it undoubtedly is, there remain intriguing challenges in this cheerfully contradictory book. Firstly, developing workshop practice is inherently about the acquisition of implicit knowledge, where one invariably learns by observing, absorbing and doing. Not everyone can attend events like the MMM Ways Into Workshop weekends, which are experiences of feeling as well as of education. But how do you get close to this through the medium of print? And how can you build the games and exercises into your practice?

Second, the practitioners featured here are constantly evolving their own techniques and creative solutions—they have learned how to fish, in the oft-quoted dictum. But the book also offers you a shoal of fish to feed on. So long as you don't try to eat them all at once, they will keep you going for a very long time. What enables Moser and the others to find their own fish, and what will enable you to do so, is the creation of a personal practice and rationale. This will come from your own history and life experience. That, and constantly remaining curious and open to new challenges.

So, with that in mind, here's the last exercise in this book, and one which I urge you to try. It's based upon the principles of 'open-source' publishing, where anyone can adopt, modify or critique other's existing work, or offer new work, without seeking permission or reward. It works on the basis that people will give of their ideas freely because they see the mutual benefit in a reciprocal process—a kind of 'all intellectual property is theft' philosophy:

> 1. Find a bunch of like-minded musicians (this is the hard part, but check out Sound Sense, Musicleader.net, or one of the other developing networks in your area).
>
> 2. Take this book along to regular mutual support sessions and try out the ideas and exercises contained here (preferably before you inflict them upon the unsuspecting public!).
>
> 3. Continue to do this until you get bored, or find that the exercises no longer meet your needs.
>
> 4. Then collectively create your own, and make widely available, so that others can repeat steps 1-4.

Bibliography and internet resources

Organisations and websites

Here are some organisations and a few websites that we have worked with or found useful. The websites all have links pages, please use them.

Asian Dub Foundation Education **www.adfed.co.uk**

Contemporary Music for Amateurs: **www.coma.org** is an organisation promoting contemporary music for amateurs with regional centres, regular performances and commissions.

Community Music: the organisation originally established by the likes of John Stevens to develop community music ideas in London, in Britain: **www.cmonline.org.uk**

Community Music East founded in the mid-1980s, still going strong: **www.cme.org**

Drake Music Project: **www.drakemusicproject.com**

Greater Manchester Music Action Zone (GMMAZ) handbook has been used extensively as a tool for Core Training days in the area. It can be found on their website at **www.gmmaz.org.uk** and includes practical material on, for instance, Do you need to apply for Disclosure?, Child Protection Guidelines, Health and Safety Guidelines, Equal Opportunities and Diversity Policy Project Planning and Co-ordination Workshop Framework and Planning Games and Exercises.

International Society for Music Education: **www.isme.org** organises an annual international conference.

www.milapfest.com South Asian Arts Festival with a range of promotions and development work.

More Music in Morecambe: **www.mormusic.net** . A vibrant website with photographs, recordings and history from all MMM projects over the years. It includes a newsflash and what's on page for MMM regular sessions and events. A number of policy documents and useful lists have been created by staff at MMM in recent years. Feel free to go to the MMM website download a document and adjust it for yourself.

MusicLeader is a professional development resource for music leaders at every stage of their career. The information and advice is collated by regional MusicLeader Networks set up and funded by national charity Youth Music as part of its nationwide MusicLeader training initiative: **www.musicleader.net**

Musical Futures: **www.phf.org.uk/musicalfutures.htm.** The Paul Hamlyn Foundation's flagship project in working toward a musical entitlement for all 11-19 year olds.

New technologies: websites for information and materials: **www.audiomulch.com** to download free software

www.emagic.de for information about Logic software.

Finale by **www.makemusic.com** and Sibelius by **www.sibelius.com** the two most popular notation software programmes, allowing you to create sheet music by entering notes using the computer typewriter keyboard, or midi instruments.

www.minidisk.org everything you ever wanted to know about MD and other formats too.

www.mp3.com a virtual music community where you can upload and download music.

www.propellerhead.se for information about Reason, ReCycle and ReBirth software .

www.steinberg.net to find out more about Cubase software.

The Sage Gateshead: works to devise, deliver and support music projects and partnerships across North East England and Cumbria. This includes an ongoing practitioner development and training programme, CoMusica (the North East Youth Music Action Zone) and Unlocking the Future, the Sage's flagship project for secondary schools: **www.thesagegateshead.org**

Sonic Arts Network: **www.sonicartsnetwork.org** a site that connects you to a massive network of national and international musicians working with new technologies.

Sound It Out is the Birmingham-based community music project: **www.sounditout.co.uk**

Sound Sense: **www.soundsense.org** National organisation supporting 'people who help make music in their communities—by leading music workshops and teaching—through a range of actions and services'. Also regularly publishes the magazine *Sounding Board: The Journal of Community Music.*

SoundStation is a fun, interactive site where young people (and their parents) can go to learn more about music, share musical experiences, get career advice and hear the latest about Youth Music initiatives in their area. It is made up of three sections, each with a different look and feel to appeal to different age groups between 0-18: **www.soundstation.org.uk**

Welfare State International: **www.welfare-state.org** A company of artists who pioneer new approaches to the arts of celebration and ceremony in Britain and internationally.

Youth Music funds and facilitates music-making for young people up to the age of 18, particularly those living in areas of social and economic need. Its funding criteria and application forms are all available online: **www.youthmusic.org.uk**

Reading recommended by the contributors in this book

Ayre, Lane. 2001. *Unintentional Music: Releasing Your Deepest Creativity.* Hampton Roads. A fascinating approach to teaching music based on process work approaches, using 'mistakes' as the road in to musical and creative development.

Boal, Augusto. 1992. *Games For Actors and Non-Actors.* London: Routledge. A practical compendium of exercises and activities aimed at freeing the inventive and performative spirit. Extremely valuable in group work. From a political theatrical background.

Bailey, Derek. [1980] 1993. *Improvisation: Its Nature and Practice in Music.* Da Capo Press. Free guitarist Bailey's history of improvisation in music, from jazz to flamenco, including interviews with many practitioners.

Bell, Clive. 1999. *'A Brief History of the London Musicians' Collective'.* **www.l-m-c.org.uk/archive/history/html**. Fascinating history of the most successful musicians' collective in Britain, responsible for outstanding improvised music events since the mid-1970s.

Cardew, Cornelius, ed. 1972. *Scratch Music.* London: Latimer. Avant-garde composer and political activist Cardew's provocative and inspiring ideas for music-making.

Chernoff, John Miller. 1979. *African Rhythms and Sensibility: Aesthetics and Social Action in African Musical Idioms*. Chicago: University of Chicago Press. An exploration of the place of rhythm music making in traditional West African culture, looking at it as a metaphor for the healthy functioning of communities.

Coult, Tony and Baz Kershaw, eds. 1999. *Engineers of the Imagination: The Welfare State Handbook.* London: Methuen. Revised edition. History and practical guidance on how to do processions and street performances, from costumes to music making, based on Welfare State International's experience.

Eames, Charles and Ray Eames. *Powers of Ten: A Flipbook (Dealing with the Relative Size of Things in the Universe and the Effects of Adding Another Zero).* New York: W.H. Freeman. An inspiring and fun way of understanding how much is going on at any one time (for instance, the intrapsychic, the interpersonal, the group).

Eno, Brian. 1996. *A Year With Swollen Appendices.* London: Faber. Eno's diary for a year, interesting enough in itself as a contemporary musical thinker, and the appendices are an added bonus of delights covering 'improvising', 'role play', 'new ways of singing' and 'sharing music' and many more.

Everitt, Anthony. 1997. *Joining In: An Investigation into Participatory Music.* London: Calouste Gulbenkian Foundation. Excellent wide-ranging report, full of information about community music, orchestral outreach projects, and so on, in Britain, as well as advocating continued support for these activities.

Finnegan, Ruth. 1989. *The Hidden Musicians: Music-making in an English Town.* Cambridge: Cambridge University Press. An analysis of all the amateur music-making that took place within a year in Milton Keynes in the 1990s. Very interesting in terms of ownership of the music ,and covers genres from church choirs, symphony orchestras, jazz groups and teenage rock bands.

Fox, John. 2002. *Eyes on Stalks.* London: Methuen. Welfare State International's director Fox's account of the performance and ritual company's history and philosophy from the late 1960s on.

Green, Lucy. *How Popular Musicians Learn: A Way Ahead for Music Education.* Aldershot: Ashgate. Advocates the use of informal learning processes—deployed for years by pop musicians—in the formal curriculum.

Hart, Mickey, and Jay Stevens. 1990. *Drumming at the Edge of Magic.* London: HarperCollins. Autobiography of one of the drummers of the Grateful Dead, also writes about the power of percussion and the drum, as well as how he runs music workshops at summer camps.

Higgins, Lee, ed. 2000. *Community Music and New Technology: 1999 Conference Report and Reflections.* Liverpool: LIPA. Collection of short essays on the subject, exploring various   practices and projects using technologies.

Houston, Gaie. 1990. *The Red Book of Gestalt.* Rochester Press. How to set up and run a group. Although from a therapeutic perspective, it has some very useful ides and hints in it that could be applied in any group.

Hunt, Peter. *Voiceworks*. Oxford: Oxford University Press. Collection of songs and useful advice for singing projects for schools, youth groups, community choirs.

Ings, Richard, Ruth Jones and Nick Randell. *Mapping Hidden Talent.* Youth Work Press. The first study of pop youth music projects in Britain.

Jencks, Charles and Nathan Silver. 1973. *Adhocism: The Case for Improvisation.* New York: Anchor. A classic about the spirit of improvisation across all culture, not only music, with a strong visual and design element.

Katundu, K. Wonganui. 1991. 'Music Education and Community needs'. In John Drummond, ed. *The Community Musician: Training a New Professional.* Pub. by the Norwegian affiliation of International Society for Music Education. An essay that relates the contemporary western 'community music' with some non-Western societies' natural incorporation of music into life and culture. The whole book has many interesting essays detailing the rise of the community music scene fifteen years ago.

Kelly, Owen. 1984. *Community Art and the State: Storming the Citadels.* London: Comedia. Classic early political account of theory and practice of community arts in Britain.

Kershaw, Baz. 1992. *The Politics of Performance: Political Theatre as Cultural Intervention.* London: Routledge, 2001. Academic account of processions, rituals, and community theatre companies in Britain.

Linklater, Kristin. *Freeing the Natural Voice.* Drama Books. A really practical voice development manual, originally written for actors, with a strong philosophical basis from which it's easy to generate new exercises and activities.

McKay, George. 2005. *Circular Breathing: The Cultural Politics of Jazz in Britain.* Durham, NC: Duke University Press. A cultural history of improvised music from the Original Dixieland Jazz Band's first 1919 London performances on, with emphasis on social and political issues in the various scenes.

Newman, P. 1998. *Therapeutic Voicework: Principles and Practice for the Use of Singing as a Therapy.* Jessica Kingsley Publishers. Wide-ranging, often fascinating, worth looking at if your interest is singing and/or therapy.

Paton, Rod. 2000. *Living Music: Improvisation Guidelines for Teachers and Community Musicians.* West Sussex County Council. Accounts and exercises about the use of improvisation in music education.

Pavlicevic, M. and Ansdell, G. eds. *Community Music Therapy.* Jessica Kingsley Publishers. Contributions from international practitioners, looking at different models of music therapy and community music.

Ristad, Eloise. 1982. *A Soprano on Her Head.* Real People Press. A visionary approach to freeing the performer inside people, told through stories of particular pieces of work the author engaged in.

Runswick, Daryl. *Rock, Jazz and Pop Arranging.* London: Faber. An 'old stand-by' of Martin's, highly practical and useful generally, not just for community music work.

Singleton, John. 2001. *The Creative Writing Workbook.* Palgrave. A book of creative writing workshop exercises and tasks from an huge array of starting points that can be translated for musical activities either alone or in groups.

Stevens, John, Julia Doyle and Ollie Crooke. 1985. *Search and Reflect: A Music Workshop Handbook*. London: Community Music. Spontaneous Music Ensemble drummer and educationalist Stevens' groundbreaking collection of exercises for improvisation, listening and rhythmic awareness, that formed the basis of the organisation Community Music early practice in the 1980s.

Storr, A. 1997. *Music and the Mind*. London: Harper Collins. Interesting exploration of the psychological value of music, even if it leans towards music = classical somewhat.

Toop, David. 1996. *Ocean of Sound*. London: Serpent's Tail. A glorious journey through twentieth century music and the rise of 'ambient music', but in particular through looking at the fusion of non-Western and Western music that (Toop argues) began with Debussy.

Tuckman, B.W. 1965. *'Developmental sequences in small groups'. Psychological Bulletin 63* (6): pp. 384-399. The original source of 'forming, norming, storming…', as usefully employed in workshop situations.

Wigram, Tony. 2004. *Improvisation: Methods and Techniques for Music Therapy Clinicians, Educators and Students*. Jessica Kingsley Publishers. Detailed account, includes recorded examples on CD but also quite a lot of notation.

Wlmer, Val. 1977. *As Serious As Your Life: The Story of the New Jazz*. London: Quartet. English jazz historian's account of the predominantly African American free scene of the 1960s and 1970s.

Wishart, Trevor. 1975. *Sound Fun: A Book of Musical Games*. Also volume 2. Universal. Set of workshop games described pictorially, some very musically complicated, but all very sonically exciting and fun.

Other references and sources through the book

Bayton, Mavis. 1998. *Frock Rock: Women Performing Popular Music*. Oxford: Oxford University Press.

Cahill, Anne. 1998. T*he Community Music Handbook: A Practical Guide to Developing Music Projects and Organisations.* Australia: Currency Press.

Carr, Ian. 1973. *Music Outside: Contemporary Jazz in Britain*. London: Latimer.

Collins, John. 1985. *African Pop Roots*. London: Foulsham.

Hayes, Jennie. 2004. Published research on community artists and participatory culture. *Mailout* magazine, January 2004.

Higham, Ben. 1990. 'Community Music: Philosophy and Practice Put to the Test'. **www.cme.org.uk/library.html**

Hutnyk, John. 2000. *Critique of Exotica: Music, Politics and the Culture Industry*. London: Pluto.

Jordison, Sam. 2003. Nomination for Morecambe as Crap Town. **www.idler.co.uk/html/frontsection/craptown/30_5/england.htm**

Lancashire County Council. 2002. *A Cultural Strategy for Lancashire*. Draft. Preston: Lancashire County Council.

Manning, Heidi. Community musician. **www.comusic.freeserve.co.uk**

Moser, Pete. 2002. 'Z-A of Community Music: Dhamak Collective'. Interview with Jane Clothier. *Sounding Board: Music Work With People.* (Autumn 2002): p9.

Peggie, Andrew. 2002. *Tuning Up: A New Look at Instrumental Music Teaching.* Stowmarket: Sound Sense.

Prévost, Eddie. 1995. *No Sound is Innocent: AMM and the Practice of Self-Invention: Meta-Musical Narratives: Essays.* Harlow: Copula.

Price, Dave. 2002. '"A quiet revolution": An Overview of Current Community Music Initiatives in the UK'. Paper given at International Society of Music Education's Community Music Activity seminar, Rotterdam Conservatory of Music and Dance, August 2002. Proceedings published: **www.cdime-network.com/cma/conference/ 021230175048483221**

Sorrell, Neil. 1992. 'Improvisation'. In John Paynter, Tim Howell, Richard Orton and Peter Seymour, eds. *Companion To Contemporary Musical Thought, vol. 2*. London: Routledge.

White, Vicky. 2004. Community music researcher. **www.communitymusic.50megs.com/custom2.html**

Notes on contributors

Dan Fox is a multi-instrumentalist, composer and designer. He was educated on the road by Welfare State International with whom he still does a couple of music projects each year. He spent five years with Dogtroep in Amsterdam, toured on Walk The Plank's first voyage, and has been involved in many MMM projects. He currently co-directs Hands On Rhythm, based in Cumbria, whose work includes commissioned sound tracks for outdoor spectacles, interactive sound installations and the manufacture of percussion instruments as used by their Youth Music Action Zone project, Boom Dang. He also plays trombone with Anglo/Dutch brass and percussion quartet Salt and started the stilt percussion/turntable band Boneshaker.

Rachel Healey is a singer, workshop leader, and evaluator of community music projects. She worked for two years in the Education department of Sonic Arts Network under Paul Wright, organising workshops in schools and the community by artists using new technologies. She had a brief career as a drum n bass DJ, put on a few spectacular house parties in Leeds, and has pursued a passion for Indian music since 1998. She has a MMus in Ethnomusicology from SOAS, University of London, and is now apprenticed to Jill Rakusen, founder of Giving Voice, an approach to the strategic use of song.

Steve Lewis is an improviser who works with voice and percussion. He has a wealth of experience in education and community arts as well as performing improvised and African music and torch songs. In the past he was a regular contributor to *The Wire* magazine. Steve has worked for MMM for many years as a performer and teacher. His current interests are in environmental percussion, instant song, leftfield pop, cross-arts collaboration and solo performance. His music work is informed by his other life as a UKCP registered psychotherapist with over 10 years experience of working with individuals, couples and groups.

George McKay is Professor of Cultural Studies at the University of Central Lancashire. He has written extensively about the cultural politics of popular music, from trad jazz to rave, and about protest and alternative cultural formations. Among his books are *Senseless Acts of Beauty: Cultures of Resistance since the Sixties* (1996), ed. *DiY Culture: Party & Protest in Nineties Britain* (1998), *Glastonbury: A Very English Fair (2000),* and he is co-editor of *Social Movement Studies: Journal of Social, Cultural and Political Protest.* His book *Circular Breathing: The Cultural Politics of Jazz in Britain* is published by Duke University Press in 2005. Prior to academia he worked for the first few years of Community Music East in Norwich, and he still plays improvising double bass a bit. **www.uclan.ac.uk/facs/class/ humanities/staff/mckay.htm**

A musical maverick who rebelled against music as taught at school, **Martin Milner** has followed his own path inspired by a passion for music making with people. This has led, at various times to jobs as classroom music teacher, lecturer, education officer for a live music venue, workshop facilitator, music project manager, and composer/ music director for theatre. As a freelancer he has worked with all sorts of groups, leading workshops and training others to do so, and written articles for community music publications. He lives in Manchester with two children, two goldfish and too many guitars.

Pete Moser is a composer, performer and teacher and has been the director of More Music in Morecambe for the past ten years. He has written scores for many theatre, opera and dance projects as well as songs for occasions and large-scale choral pieces such as *Start Again,* a celebration of the Universal Declaration of Human Rights. He is a multi-instrumentalist and teaches percussion, voice, brass and songwriting, as well as the art of running workshops. He has written occasional articles about these topics. He is an experienced initiator and manager of projects as well as the Fastest-One-Man-Band-In-The-World.

Hugh Nankivell is a freelance composer, performer and educator and is based in Huddersfield. He has regular, creative music adventures with Opera North, at Huddersfield University, at Lydgate Special School, with his own band Nankivell's Optet, and with the community band Dangerous Volume. He also composes at least one song per week and makes soundtracks for the puppetry theatre company Faulty Optic and he specialises in creating group compositions. Hugh plays musical games whenever and wherever he can.

David Price has been involved in the community music scene in the UK for over 20 years and has also worked extensively in the formal education sector. He was project leader at the Abraham Moss Centre, Head of Performing Arts at South Manchester College and then as the Director of Learning at the Liverpool Institute of Performing Arts devised a unique curricular framework for vocational studies. He currently works as a consultant, specialising in music, education and training, and is project leader for the Paul Hamlyn Foundation 'Musical Futures' project.

Lemn Sissay is a Northwest poet with a national reputation. Fusing the lyrical and the polemical, up beat humour and deadly seriousness, his work is known for its powerful energy and dynamism. He has published several books, recorded with a number of jazz-fusion outfits, and worked extensively in television and radio. According to *The Big Issue*, Lemn's work is 'Fierce, funny, serious, satirical streetwise and tender'.

Katherine Zeserson has been working with voices for 25 years, and has a national reputation as a vocal trainer, creative workshop facilitator and community educator. She has taught voice, music, performance and community arts skills in education settings from nursery to degree level; and led creative projects in the broadest range of community and arts contexts, working with anxious beginners as well as professional performers, and all points in between. She is a performer of jazz, improvised, contemporary and traditional song and is Director of Community Music for The Sage Gateshead.

CL